DUFFER
I0818986

JAMIE OLIVER

GRILL

Photography DAVID LOFTUS

Design JAMES VERITY

appetite
by RANDOM HOUSE

DEDICATED TO

Skye Gyngell

1963 — 2025

There are many things I greatly admired about Skye Gyngell – her good heart, her deep understanding of the seasons, and her humble approach to celebrating ingredients, to name just a few. Her cooking felt effortless, though there was much thought behind it. Her dishes were both elegant and understated, with simplicity at their core. Skye was one of the matriarchs of truly beautiful, modern food, and a lot can be learnt from her. It would have been a dream come true to work with Skye in some way, but many of my Fifteen students were lucky enough to be blessed by her mentorship and employment – she believed in hope and transformation for young souls in the industry. Her love and influence will be felt for generations to come.

Contents

Embrace the seasons & get grilling!

DUFFER

The joy of getting outdoors, in every season, in any weather, lighting that grill and cooking in the open air is something I'd love everyone to experience. So, with this book, I want to empower you with the confidence, skills and recipes to do just that.

If you're a beginner griller, you'll find that with a bit of know-how, curiosity and courage, you can craft all sorts of remarkable meals. And if you're a seasoned faithful, searching for new inspiration, I'm confident you'll find that in these pages.

This isn't a book for bravado or bluster. This is about practical skills, solid recipes and plenty of tips so you can light, tend and grill with efficiency and a calm outlook.

Grilling is a wonderfully intuitive way to cook and can bring extraordinary flavor and texture to the most humble of ingredients. Here, you'll discover how to make vegetables sing with crispness and sweet char, you'll find new wonder in delicately smoking and steaming fish, you'll meet beautiful burgers – but not as you know them – and you'll uncover an array of wonderful ways to accent, grill and serve up cuts of meat. I've also included a handful of irresistible brunch bits, and those all-important supporting-actor recipes that help to make your whole grill experience rock.

Cooking over flame is uplifting for the soul

It's about forging memories, nourishing gatherings and tasting something real. I truly believe that managing fire is written into our DNA somehow.

From South Africa's braais and America's phenomenal pitmasters to communal grilling in Korea. From smoky fire cooking in Japan over carbonized branches to Navajo cooking techniques, the heart of the story is the same. Cooking over fire has the ability to bring people together in a way that the latest kitchen technology never could.

Grilling isn't just about what's on your plate

It's a primal ritual that has the ability to stir something deep within us all. Taming flames, reading the coals and orchestrating the heat is as mesmerizing as watching a sunset blaze and fade or feeling the power of a waterfall. You have to use your intuition, to learn how to respond and react, moving things around to get the best from the grill. Once you're in the groove, you'll find it's ever so satisfying.

Mastery of fire belongs to everyone

And the magic is in realizing that the grill can be for every day of the year. Fire can warm a cold blue-sky morning or transform a rainy afternoon. Roast or braise on the barbecue, even on Christmas Day, and you'll enjoy delicious, surprising results. From meals in under 30 minutes to weekend feasts, whether it's everyday cooking or hosting friends and family, I want to help you have a stress-free experience.

So let's reclaim the grill as a gathering place for food, family, friendship, gratitude and that beautiful depth of flavor that only grilling can bring.

Welcome to the heart & art of grilling

Get ready to grill

OH WISE ONE
TRADE
MARK
SAFETY MATCHES

Getting your grill area in order before you start cooking is key in setting you up for success

For me, the skill comes from being organized, planning ahead and understanding the core techniques and protocols that will serve you well. So, take a moment to think about what you'll be cooking and what equipment you'll need, meaning you can focus on the grilling, rather than running around in a panic looking for things!

I find it helpful to have a folding table, chair or crate on either side of the grill, one for raw ingredients and food that's prepped and ready to cook, and one for your cooked stuff, so you can keep things organized and avoid cross-contamination.

Remember, every grill is different, and the perfect "setup" is the one that makes it the easiest and the safest for you. Don't worry what it looks like – if it works, it works!

Things to consider for the prep side

- Matches and natural firestarters to get things going
- Wood chips for adding extra smokiness and depth of flavor
- Long-handled tongs to put things safely on the grill and turn them while cooking
- Gloves to protect your hands from the heat
- A cutting board and chef's knife for easy prep
- Sea salt and black pepper for seasoning
- Olive oil, red wine vinegar and water in spray bottles, allowing you to be attentive to your food as it cooks and have control of how much you use

And over on the cooked side

- A digital food thermometer to ensure your meat is perfectly cooked
- Long-handled tongs or a spatula to remove cooked food from the grill
- Serving boards and platters ready to dish up
- Extra virgin olive oil, for finishing dishes
- Staple pantry items like olive oil, extra virgin olive oil, red wine vinegar, sea salt and black pepper pop up regularly but aren't included in individual ingredients lists

It's also good practice to have on hand

- A decent grill brush to use before, during and after cooking
- A bowl of hot soapy water to keep your hands clean
- A garbage bin or bowl to keep any waste in one place
- A fire extinguisher or fire blanket, to be safe

In terms of additional equipment, I'd also recommend the following

- A chimney starter (read more on page 16)
- Long metal or wooden skewers (just remember to soak wooden skewers before use, to prevent them burning when on the grill)
- Cast-iron pans, particularly a shallow Dutch oven, a large deep pan and a small frying pan
- Enamel pans, dishes and bowls that you can put directly on the grill

Grill setup

Charcoal, gas or electric?

I'm a big fan of cooking over fire, so a charcoal grill will always win out for me. Once you get to know your grill and get in the zone, you'll find it's easy to use and a fairly clean heat source without too much smoke. Please choose sustainably and ideally locally sourced charcoal or briquettes with no nasty chemicals. Generally, the better the quality, the longer the coals will burn for, so it's worth upgrading if you can.

Gas can be very convenient, just turn it on, let it preheat, and go, and it can be a more sustainable option than charcoal. If cooking on gas, use the temperature knobs to adjust the heat across your grill to create hot, medium and cool zones that echo the charcoal setups I've detailed in the book (pages 18–19). If you want to add wood chips to your gas grill to create smokiness, simply use a smoker box or metal tray, placed directly on the grates of the grill. Finally there are electric grills, which definitely seem to be on the up. They're the most sustainable option of all, and can be very helpful if you live somewhere with limited outdoor space.

How to light your chimney starter

With charcoal grilling, I really recommend using a chimney starter – it will make your grill life a lot easier. Chimneys are useful as they mean you can light your coals in an even way, but also because they light quickly. I find it easiest to remove the grate from the grill, place the chimney inside over a lit firestarter, and start it there. Once the coals are glowing amber at the top and covered with a fine layer of gray ash, carefully tip them out and use a grill brush or long-handled tongs to drag or push the hot coals to exactly where you want them. Put the grate back over the coals, and put the hot chimney somewhere safe to cool down. Once the coals and grate are in place, I like to pop the lid on for 5 minutes before I start cooking – I find it helps the bars of the grate to heat up. Check out pages 18–19 to learn more about the different coal setups and why they're useful, and on each recipe in this book you'll see I've recommended the best coal setup to use.

Using the vents for heat control

You'll see that often in recipes where you cook with the grill lid on, I also say to have the vents open. The vents are there to help you regulate the airflow in your grill – the ones at the bottom let air in to fuel the fire, and the ones at the top allow heat to escape. Having the vents open means you get a stronger heat, speeding up your cooking. Occasionally I recommend having the top vent only half open – this is generally for instances where it is helpful to keep the coals going for longer, like with slow-cooked meats. Where possible – and this will vary from model to model – it's good practice to have the vents open on the opposite side to the hot coals.

Cleaning your grill

It's important to give your grill a bit of love, and that means investing in a good grill brush and using it before, during and after grilling to keep the grate clean and prevent whatever it is you're cooking from sticking. Don't skip this step!

Good practice for charcoal grilling

Once you've finished grilling, close the vents to stop the coals or briquettes burning. Next time you fill your chimney starter, knock any ash off the outside of these half-used coals or briquettes and add them in with the fresh ones to light and use again. This saves waste and a bit of money, too! Before you light the chimney, clear out any old ash from the bottom of your grill – you don't want to get a build-up there as it can block the air vents, affecting the airflow and success of your grilling.

Coal setups

Graduated

With this setup, you want to have your coals starting high at one side, creating a fierce hot zone, and gradually sloping down to a single layer of a few coals at the other, creating medium and cool zones along the way. This allows you to have maximum control over your grilling, moving food between the zones to speed up or slow down cooking as you need to.

Flat

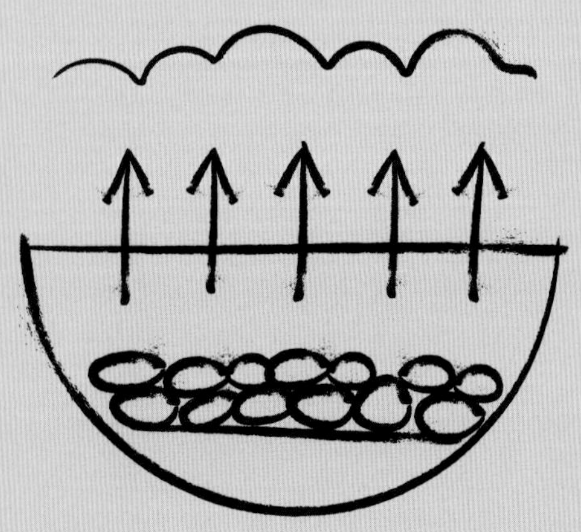

You guessed it, this is about a flat level of coals across the bottom of the grill, meaning you're ready for consistent grilling. There's no cool zone, so you need to remember to be attentive to whatever you're cooking.

50/50

Simply pile all your coals evenly into one half of the grill, leaving the other half clear. This gives you a clear hot zone and cool zone, with a medium area in the middle where you can get the best of both worlds. This setup is helpful for recipes where you need to sear or get something going over direct heat, but then want to give it time to cook through more gently over indirect heat.

Channel

A channel setup is useful when what you're cooking would benefit from more of an even all-round heat. It mimics cooking in an oven, allows you to cook at a slower pace, and is particularly well suited to lid-on, vents-open grilling. Arrange your coals evenly at either side of the grill, leaving a clear coal-free channel in the middle.

Cooking temperatures

For chicken, meat and fish, a digital food thermometer will be your best friend in working out when it's safe to eat. Simply probe the thickest part, which will take the longest to cook, and remember to wipe the thermometer clean after each use.

CHICKEN	For individual cuts like breasts and thighs, cook through to at least **165°F**. For whole birds, the internal temp of the breast should be **160°F** when you remove from the grill and needs to reach **165°F** after resting
PORK & SAUSAGES	For individual cuts and chops, cook through to at least **145°F**, and for sausages, cook through to **160°F**. For larger cuts, the internal temp should be at least **145°F** when you remove them from the grill and needs to reach **150°F** after resting
STEAK	For rare, remove at about **115°F**, rising to at least **120°F** after resting For medium-rare, remove at about **125°F**, rising to **130°F** after resting For medium, remove at about **135°F**, rising to **140°F** after resting For medium-well, remove at about **145°F**, rising to **150°F** after resting
BEEF	For medium, the internal temperature should be about **130°F** when you remove it from the grill, rising to **140°F** after resting, and for well done, about **150°F**, rising to **160°F** after resting
LAMB	For medium, the internal temperature should be **130°F** to **135°F** when you remove it from the grill, rising to about **140°F** after resting, and for well done, about **150°F**, rising to **160°F** after resting
FISH	The internal temperature should be at least **145°F** and the flesh opaque

Fast & impressive

Chicken escalope, smoky bacon, green veg & pesto

Serves 2 | **30 minutes**

1 lemon

1 clove of garlic

1 bunch of Italian parsley (about 1 oz)

¼ cup shelled unsalted pistachios

1 pinch of dried red chili flakes

1 oz feta cheese

4 scallions

1 head of romaine lettuce

6 oz asparagus (about ⅓ of a bunch)

1 cup frozen peas

2 x 5-oz boneless, skinless chicken breasts

2 slices of bacon

1 Finely grate and reserve the lemon zest. To make a pesto, peel and thinly slice the garlic, set half aside and pound the rest in a mortar and pestle with a pinch of sea salt. Roughly chop and add the parsley, stems and all, and bash into a coarse paste. Pound in the pistachios, then muddle in 2 tablespoons of extra virgin olive oil, squeeze in the lemon juice and add the chili flakes. Crumble in the feta and set aside (make this in a food processor, if you prefer).

2 Light the grill (pages 16–19). Cook the scallions and lettuce on the hot zone until lightly charred, turning with tongs, then transfer to your board.

3 Add the reserved sliced garlic to a cast-iron pan with 1 tablespoon of olive oil. Trim the asparagus and charred scallions, then slice with the lettuce, leaving the asparagus tips whole. Add it all to the pan with a pinch each of salt and black pepper and a splash of water, and cook for 5 minutes on the hot zone, or until softened, stirring regularly. Add the peas and reserved lemon zest, and carefully move the pan to the cool zone.

4 Use a sharp knife to carefully slice into the chicken breasts, then open each one out flat like a book, spritz with olive oil, season with salt and pepper, and grill on the hot zone for 7 to 10 minutes, or until cooked through, turning regularly with tongs. Crisp up the bacon on the cool zone.

5 Divide up the green veg and bacon, slice and add the chicken, then spoon 1 heaping tablespoon of pesto over each portion (stash the rest in the fridge for another day). Great with couscous, grains or crusty bread.

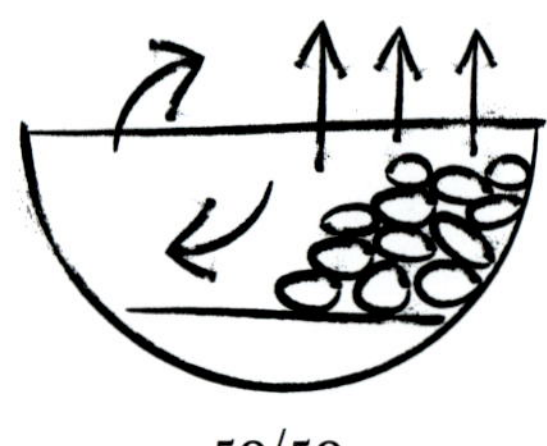

50/50

Perfect steak & chargrilled salad

Serves 2 | 20 minutes

1 x 1-inch-thick boneless strip steak (about 12 oz)

1 bunch of mixed woody herbs (about ⅔ oz), such as thyme, marjoram, rosemary

2-inch piece of ginger

1 clove of garlic

½ to 1 fresh red chili

1 tablespoon reduced-sodium soy sauce

1 tablespoon runny honey

1 lime

1 small bunch of broccolini (6 oz)

6 oz asparagus (about ⅓ of a bunch)

1 bunch of scallions

8 to 12 small radishes (about 3½ oz)

6 oz sugar snap peas

2 sprigs of mint

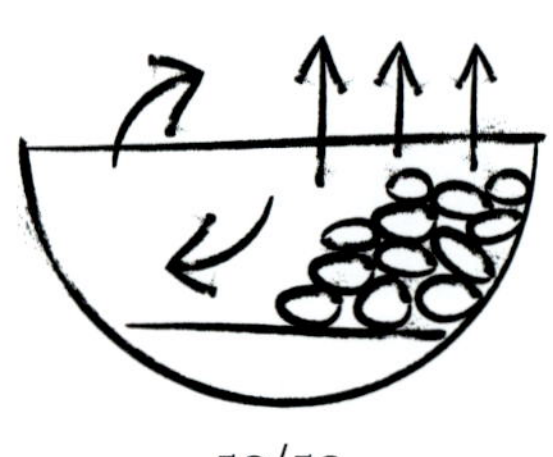

50/50

1 Get the steak out of the fridge to come to room temperature. Light the grill (pages 16–19). Make a herb brush by tying the woody herbs to the end of a wooden spoon with a piece of string. Peel and finely grate the ginger and garlic into a large bowl, then finely grate in the chili. Add the soy and honey and squeeze in the lime juice. Set aside.

2 Remove the fat from the steak, discarding the sinew, then thinly slice the fat and add to a small cast-iron frying pan. Put it on the cool zone to render and crisp up. Season the steak all over with sea salt. Place it on the hot zone, turning with tongs to cook gently on all sides, or until gnarly, using the herb brush to baste it with the rendered fat as you go – you'll need 2 minutes for rare (or until 115°F), 3 minutes for medium-rare (or until 125°F) and 4 minutes for medium (or until 135°F). Transfer to a plate to rest – if you're using a thermometer, the temperature should go up about 5 degrees as it rests.

3 Trim the broccolini, asparagus and scallions and place on the hot zone along with the radishes. Cook for 5 minutes, or until tender and charred, turning regularly with tongs and transferring to the bowl of dressing once done. Trim the sugar snaps, pile into a metal sieve and place on the medium zone for 2 minutes, tossing occasionally, then add to the bowl, along with the crispy bits of steak fat, if you like. Toss well and transfer to a serving platter.

4 Slice the steaks and arrange on top, drizzling with any resting juices, then pick and sprinkle on the mint leaves, to serve.

Lamb lollipops, whipped feta & pistachios

Serves 4 | 45 minutes

8 oz feta cheese

3 lemons

¼ cup shelled unsalted pistachios

12 lamb rib chops, frenched (2½ to 3 lbs total)

1 bulb of garlic

1¾ lbs new potatoes

1 tablespoon dried mint

1 tablespoon fennel seeds

½ tablespoon smoked paprika

optional: 2 sprigs of oregano

1 In a blender or a small food processor, blitz the feta with the juice of 1 lemon and 1 tablespoon of extra virgin olive oil until smooth, then season and stash in the fridge until needed. Bash the pistachios in a mortar and pestle until fine, then transfer to a small bowl. Light the grill (pages 16–19).

2 If there's excess fat on the lamb, trim off about 2 tablespoons' worth and finely chop it, then add to a large shallow cast-iron pan on the hot zone (if you don't have any excess fat, use 2 tablespoons of olive oil). Once the fat starts sizzling, smash and add the unpeeled garlic cloves, then use a vegetable peeler to add the peel of 1 lemon in strips. Stir regularly until lightly golden.

3 Wash the potatoes, chop into ¾-inch chunks, and stir into the pan. Cook for 30 minutes with the grill lid on, vents open, or until softened, stirring occasionally and adding splashes of water, if needed. Squeeze in the juice of the peeled lemon and carefully move the pan to the cool zone.

4 Meanwhile, in the mortar and pestle, pound the mint, fennel seeds, paprika and a pinch each of sea salt and black pepper until fine. Scatter across your board, then turn the lamb in the seasoning until well coated. Spritz with oil, then grill on the hot zone for 10 minutes, or until golden and gnarly, turning with tongs.

5 To serve, spread the whipped feta onto a platter and drizzle with extra virgin olive oil. Add the lamb lollipops and pick and sprinkle on the oregano, if using. Serve with the lamb-fat potatoes and lemon wedges. Use the lamb to scoop up some whipped feta, then dunk into the pistachios. Great with a simple green salad, or my Best-ever tomato salad (page 108).

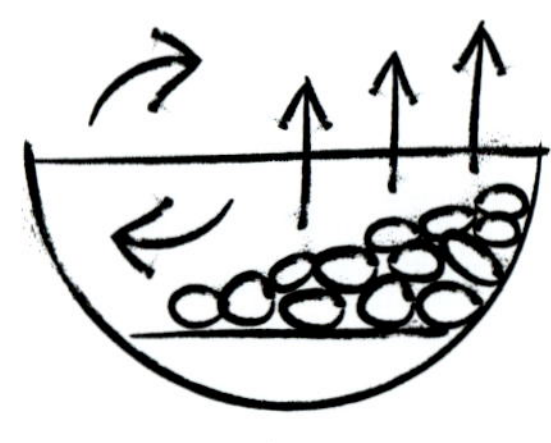

Graduated

Romesco cauliflower

Serves 4 | **35 minutes**

1 head of cauliflower (about 1¾ lbs), ideally with leaves

12 oz ripe tomatoes

4 cloves of garlic

2 slices of sourdough bread (about 3½ oz total)

1 x 16-oz jar of roasted red peppers

3 tablespoons smoked almonds, plus extra to serve

1 pinch of smoked paprika

4 sprigs of Italian parsley

1 oz feta cheese

1 Light the grill (pages 16–19). Remove and discard any shriveled outer leaves from the cauliflower, then chop it into eight wedges, spritz with olive oil, and season with sea salt and black pepper.

2 Put the cauliflower wedges and the tomatoes on the hot zone, and put the unpeeled garlic cloves on the medium zone. Place the bread on the cool zone. Cook it all with the lid on, vents open, for 10 minutes, then transfer the tomatoes, garlic and toast to your board. Flip the cauli and cook lid on, vents open, for another 10 minutes, or until charred and cooked through, moving to the medium zone if coloring too quickly.

3 Pinch off and discard the tomato skins, adding the soft insides to a blender. Squeeze in the garlic cloves, discarding the skins, and tear in the toast. Add the peppers, juices and all, along with the almonds, paprika and 2 tablespoons of extra virgin olive oil. Blitz until smooth, then season to perfection and spread onto your platter.

4 Place the charred cauliflower wedges on top of the sauce. Roughly chop and sprinkle on the parsley leaves and a few extra almonds, crumble on the feta and finish with a drizzle of extra virgin olive oil, if you like. Great with extra toast on the side, to mop up the excess sauce.

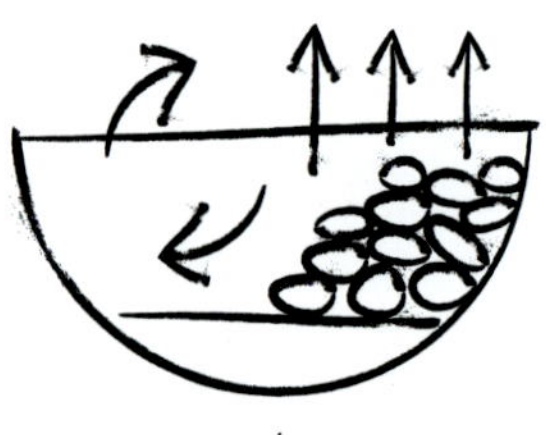

50/50

Quick beet mackerel

Serves 2 | 15 minutes

2 small raw beets (6 oz), preferably with greens attached

1½ inches fresh horseradish or 2 teaspoons jarred horseradish

2 heaping tablespoons Greek yogurt

1 lemon

2 x 3-oz mackerel fillets, skin on, scaled, pin-boned

4 sprigs of thyme

1 Light the grill (pages 16–19) and give the grate a really good brush to clean it – this will help prevent the fish from sticking.

2 Very thinly slice the beets and arrange on a nice serving board with any delicate greens. Finely grate the horseradish alongside, spoon on the yogurt and season with a little sea salt and black pepper.

3 Halve the lemon and char cut side down on the grill. Rub the fish with olive oil and season well with salt and pepper. Pick and sprinkle on the thyme, then place between the hot and medium zones, skin side down, for 2 minutes, or until the fish is nearly cooked through, moving to the medium zone if coloring too quickly, then flipping over to cook through for a final minute.

4 Use tongs to squeeze half the charred lemon over the board, then place the fish on top and drizzle with a little extra virgin olive oil, if you like. Serve with the remaining lemon, for squeezing over. Great with My favorite focaccia (page 226) or Med-style greens (page 92).

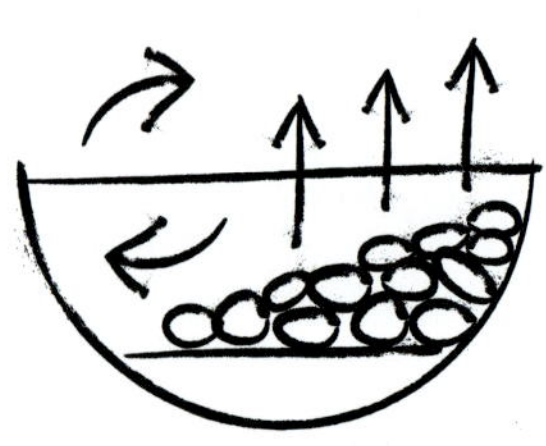

Graduated

Lemon-steamed fish & charred greens

Serves 2 | **30 minutes**

1 lb green veg, such as romanesco, asparagus, scallions, fava beans in their pods, snow peas, cabbage

2 lemons

8 Swiss chard or cabbage leaves

2 x 5-oz branzino or black sea bass fillets, skin on, scaled, pin-boned

1 x 2-oz tin of anchovy fillets in oil, drained

optional: a few sprigs of soft herbs, such as chives and dill

¼ cup mayo (or make your own, page 210)

Delicate white fish contrasts beautifully with the depth of flavor of charred veg in this ever-so-beautiful dinner for two. Use a flavored mayo for an extra dimension, or go all out and make your own (page 210).

1 Light the grill (pages 16–19). Trim the green veg as needed, cutting the romanesco into small florets, if using. Give it all a wash and gently shake dry, retaining some residual moisture. Grill the veg until softened and lightly charred, turning regularly with tongs, and transferring to a large bowl as it's done – if you have one, a wire rack placed on top of the grate will prevent smaller veg from falling through. Toss with the juice of ½ a lemon and ½ tablespoon of extra virgin olive oil and set aside.

2 Briefly warm the chard leaves on the grill for a few seconds, then remove and spritz with water. Lay out two pairs of overlapping leaves, and place a fish fillet skin side down on each pair. Spritz with olive oil and season with sea salt and black pepper, then thinly slice ½ a lemon and lay it on top. Cover with the remaining leaves, then place on the grill to steam with the lid on, vents open, for 10 minutes, or until the fish is beautifully cooked through.

3 Lay the anchovies on a plate, squeeze on the juice of ½ a lemon, drizzle with extra virgin olive oil, and pick and sprinkle on a few soft herbs, if using.

4 Divide the dressed veg among your plates, then place the delicately cooked fish on top, discarding the leaves. Dollop on the mayo, add a few dressed anchovies, and tuck in, squeezing on extra lemon, to taste.

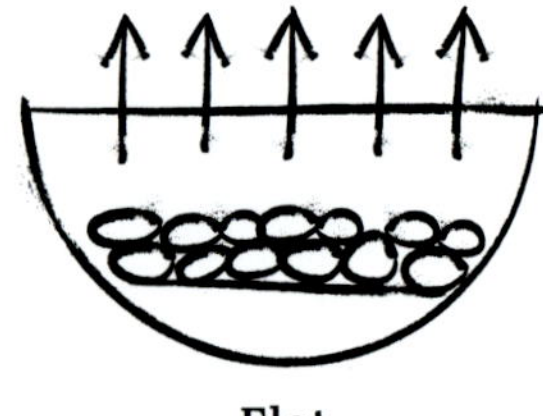

Flat

Seared carpaccio of beef

Serves 4 | 15 minutes, plus marinating

1½ lbs top sirloin roast

½ a bunch of woody herbs (about ⅓ oz), such as rosemary, thyme

1 teaspoon fennel seeds

½ x 2-oz tin of anchovy fillets in oil

½ to 1 fresh red chili

2 teaspoons English or Dijon mustard

3 tablespoons mayo (or make your own, page 210)

1 lemon

12 oz ripe cherry tomatoes, on the vine

scant 1 cup baby arugula

1 Cut off and discard any fat and sinew from the beef, then place it in a small roasting pan. Strip the herb leaves into a mortar and pestle, add the fennel seeds and a good pinch each of sea salt and black pepper, and pound into a paste. Muddle in 1 tablespoon of olive oil, then rub all over the meat. Cover and let marinate for 1 hour.

2 Lay the anchovies on a plate, drizzle with 1 tablespoon each of red wine vinegar and extra virgin olive oil, then thinly slice and add the chili. In a small bowl, mix the mustard into the mayo, then stir in squeezes of lemon juice until you have a drizzleable consistency. Light the grill (pages 16–19).

3 Grill the vines of tomatoes on the hot zone until softened and the skins start to split, turning with tongs and transferring to a bowl once done. Sear the beef on the hot zone for 1 minute on each side, turning with tongs, then transfer to a clean board to rest for 1 minute.

4 Use the whole length of a large sharp knife to very thinly slice the beef, then lay the slices across your board, sprinkle with a little salt, to taste, pick and scatter on the tomatoes, add pinches of arugula and the anchovies, then drizzle with the lemony mustard mayo. Great as it is, or simply with good crusty bread.

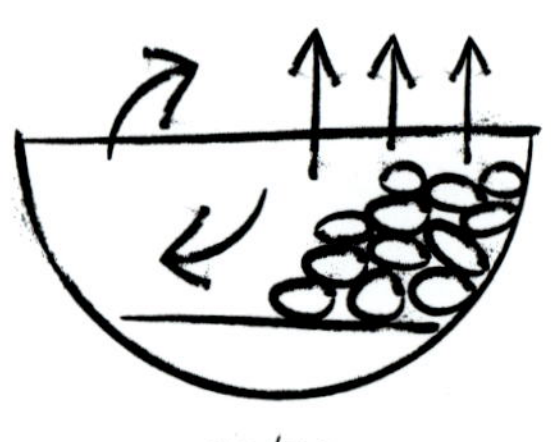

50/50

Chicken skewers & Tuscan bread salad

Serves 6 | 40 minutes

2 zucchini

2 mixed-color bell peppers

4 x 5-oz boneless, skinless chicken breasts

12 fresh bay leaves

2 lemons

8 slices of bacon

2½ lbs ripe mixed-color tomatoes

1 large loaf of ciabatta

1 big bunch of basil (about 2 oz)

⅔ cup ricotta cheese

1 Light the grill (pages 16–19). To make the skewers, chop the zucchini, peppers and chicken into scant 1-inch chunks, discarding the pepper seeds and stems. Add to a large bowl with the bay. Finely grate in the zest of 1 lemon and squeeze in the juice, then halve the remaining lemon, thinly slice half of it and add to the bowl. Add 2 tablespoons of olive oil and a pinch each of sea salt and black pepper and toss together well.

2 Load everything up onto skewers, alternating as you go, and weaving the bacon in between it all, being mindful not to pack it on too tightly.

3 Cook the skewers on the hot zone for 10 to 15 minutes, or until golden and cooked through, turning and spritzing regularly with oil and vinegar, and moving to the medium or cool zones if they're coloring too quickly. Once done, transfer to a platter and squeeze on the remaining lemon juice.

4 Reserving 2 larger tomatoes, place the rest on the medium zone for 5 minutes, or until blistered and softened, turning once, then transfer to a board. Halve the ciabatta lengthwise and crisp up on the cool zone.

5 Halve the reserved tomatoes and grate them cut side down into a serving bowl, discarding the skin. Add 1 teaspoon of red wine vinegar and 2 tablespoons of extra virgin olive oil and season to perfection. Pick and add the basil.

6 Roughly pinch off and discard the skins of the grilled tomatoes, chop the toasted bread, and toss both into the dressing. Spoon in the ricotta and gently mix together. To serve, run a sharp knife down the length of the skewers, so everything tumbles onto the platter, and get stuck in.

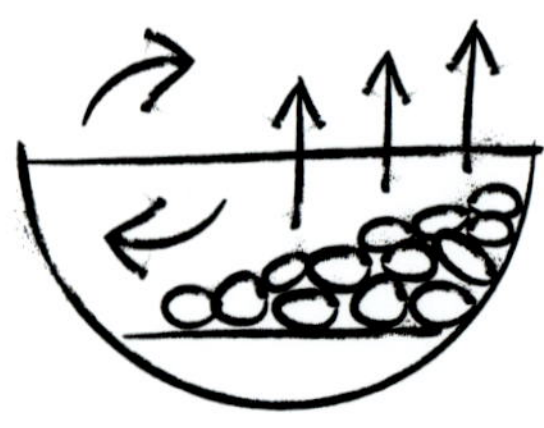

Graduated

Grilled fish tacos & stone fruit salsa

Serves 4 | 45 minutes

4 scallops, trimmed and roes removed, with the shells

4 tablespoons unsalted butter, at room temperature

4 sprigs of thyme

smoked paprika, for dusting

1¼ lbs stone fruit, such as apricots, plums

3 mixed-color chilies

4 scallions

½ a bunch of cilantro (about ½ oz)

1 lime

1 x 12-oz steelhead trout fillet, skin on, scaled

4 x 3-oz mackerel fillets, skin on, scaled, pin-boned

12 small corn tortillas

4 tablespoons sour cream

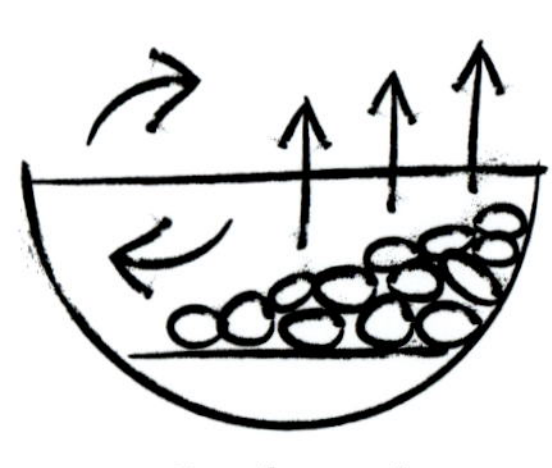

Graduated

1 Light the grill (pages 16–19). Soak a handful of wood chips according to the package instructions.

2 Score crosshatches into the scallops, going halfway through. Divide the butter among the shells, then top with the scallops, pick and sprinkle on the thyme and dust with a little paprika (if you don't have shells, place the scallops in a small cast-iron pan).

3 Halve and pit the fruit and place cut side down on the medium-hot zone. Prick and add the whole chilies, along with the scallions. Grill for 5 minutes, or until soft and charred, transferring to a board as you go. Give the grate a good brush to clean it.

4 Halve and seed the chilies, trim the scallions, and finely chop it all with the fruit and the cilantro, stems and all, mixing as you go. Squeeze on the juice of ½ a lime, add 1 tablespoon of extra virgin olive oil and season to perfection.

5 Drain the wood chips and place on the hot zone. Season the trout with sea salt and cook skin side down on the medium zone with the lid on, vents open, for 5 minutes, then add the mackerel skin side down alongside, and add the scallops in their shells (or in the cast-iron pan) to the hot zone. Cook lid on, vents open, for another 5 minutes, moving the scallops to the cool zone after 3 minutes, until firm, opaque and cooked through (about another 3 minutes). Once the mackerel and trout are done, transfer them to a board, then carefully pull off the trout skin and return it to the grill to crisp up.

6 Briefly warm the tortillas on the grill, then load up with the fish and scallops, stone fruit salsa, crispy skin and sour cream. Nice with lime-dressed avo and shredded cabbage, a few soft herb leaves, and some extra lime wedges.

Herby eggplant & zingy feta flatbreads

Serves 2 | **30 minutes**

8 oz feta cheese

1 pinch of dried red chili flakes

1 pinch of dried oregano

2 lemons

½ a bunch of mint (about ½ oz)

½ a bunch of Italian parsley (about ½ oz)

2 heaping tablespoons shelled unsalted pistachios

2 tablespoons drained capers

1 tablespoon runny honey

2 small eggplants (8 oz each)

2 flatbreads (or make your own, page 228)

3 oz mixed salad greens (about 3 cups)

½ a pomegranate

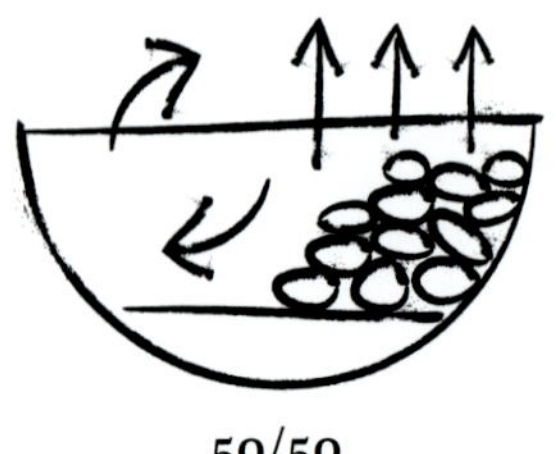

50/50

1 Light the grill (pages 16–19). Soak a handful of wood chips according to the package instructions. Place the feta in a small enamel dish, drizzle with 1 tablespoon of olive oil and sprinkle with the chili flakes and oregano, then use a vegetable peeler to strip on the peel of 1 lemon.

2 To make a dressing, pick most of the mint and parsley leaves into a mortar and pestle, reserving a few nice small leaves. Add a pinch of sea salt and pound into a paste, then bash in the pistachios and capers. Finely grate in the zest of the remaining lemon, squeeze in the juice, muddle in the honey and 2 tablespoons of extra virgin olive oil, then season to perfection.

3 Drain the wood chips and place on the hot zone. Prick the whole eggplants and place on the medium zone. Cook lid on, vents open, for 20 minutes, or until the eggplants are soft and tender, turning halfway and adding the dish of feta alongside for the last 10 minutes. Briefly warm the flatbreads, or cook through, if making your own (page 228).

4 Put the flatbreads on your plates, scattering the salad greens on top. Slice open the soft eggplants, scoop out the flesh and spoon over the salad, then crumble on half the grilled feta (save the rest for salad, soup or wraps another day). Drizzle with the herby dressing and sprinkle with the reserved herb leaves. Holding the pomegranate half cut side down, bash the back with a spoon so some of the seeds tumble out over the plates, then tuck in!

Jools' salmon niçoise

Serves 2 | 40 minutes

2 large eggs

2 teaspoons Dijon mustard

4 black olives, with pits

4 anchovy fillets in oil

½ a lemon

1 bunch of chives (about ⅔ oz)

12 oz large new potatoes

8 oz mixed green beans and wax beans

8 oz baby zucchini

2 x 5-oz salmon fillets, skin on, scaled, pin-boned

1 Lower the eggs into a pan of vigorously simmering water on the stove and boil for 5½ minutes exactly, then refresh under cold water until cool enough to handle, and peel. In a large shallow serving bowl, mix the mustard with 1 tablespoon each of red wine vinegar and extra virgin olive oil, then season to perfection. Tear in the olives, discarding the pits. Halve the anchovies lengthwise, add to a small bowl and squeeze in the lemon juice. Finely chop the chives. Light the grill (pages 16–19).

2 Slice the potatoes lengthwise a scant ½ inch thick and place on the hot zone. Trim the beans and baby zucchini and place alongside. Cook lid on, vents open, for 5 to 10 minutes, or until nicely charred, turning regularly with tongs, then move it all to the cool zone and cook the potatoes for another 15 minutes, lid on, vents open, transferring the beans and zucchini straight to the bowl of dressing as they're done. Transfer the potatoes to a board.

3 Rub the salmon with olive oil and black pepper, then cook flesh side down on the medium zone for 8 to 10 minutes, lid on, vents open, or until golden and cooked through. Use tongs to pull off the skin and crisp it up alongside.

4 Chop the grilled potatoes into scant 1-inch chunks and mix into the dressing bowl with the chopped chives. Quarter and add the eggs, flake on the salmon, break on the crispy skin, and finish with the anchovies, drizzling with the lemon juice they were marinated in.

Easy swap: Feel free to use regular zucchini instead – simply quarter them lengthwise before cooking.

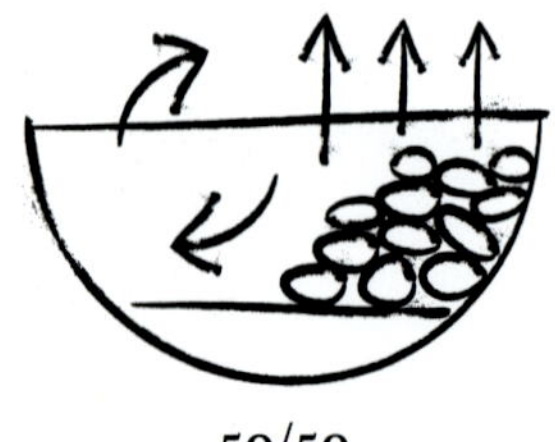

50/50

Smashed lamb wraps

Serves 4 | 30 minutes

- 1 red onion
- 2 cloves of garlic
- 1 tablespoon cumin seeds
- 1 tablespoon coriander seeds
- 1 x 8-oz jar of sun-dried tomatoes in oil
- 1 lb ground lamb
- ½ a bunch of mint (about ½ oz)
- 1 English cucumber (12 oz)
- 8 to 12 small radishes (about 3½ oz)
- 8 small flour tortillas
- ⅔ cup Greek yogurt
- 8 pickled chilies

Embracing lahmacun vibes, these wraps are a celebration of beautifully spiced juicy lamb and fresh crunchy veg. Quick to make, but ever so delicious.

1 Peel and halve the onion, placing one half in a food processor. Peel and add the garlic, along with the cumin and coriander seeds, and a pinch each of sea salt and black pepper. Drain and add the sun-dried tomatoes, and blitz until finely chopped, then pulse in the lamb until just combined.

2 Pick the mint leaves. Prep the cucumber and radishes – I've gone chunky here but feel free to thinly slice, if you prefer. Very thinly slice the remaining onion and scrunch with 1 tablespoon of red wine vinegar and a pinch of salt, then let sit to quickly pickle. Light the grill (pages 16–19).

3 Divide the lamb mixture among the tortillas, pressing it on and spreading it thinly to the edges. Spritz with olive oil and cook in batches, lamb side down, for 2 minutes, then flip and cook for just 30 seconds to 1 minute on the other side to lightly crisp up the tortillas. You can serve right away, or stack them on top of each other to keep warm.

4 To serve, layer up with the cucumber, radishes, yogurt, a little quick-pickled red onion, the mint leaves and a pickled chili. Fantastic with a generous amount of Chili sauce (page 204), too. Roll, squash and devour!

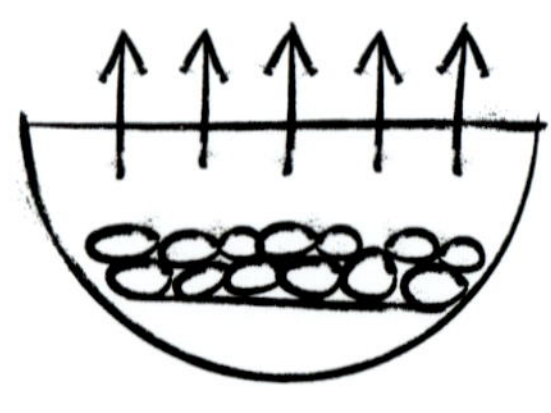

Flat

Citrus chili tofu, greens & chickpea rice

Serves 4 | **25 minutes, plus marinating**

- 1 lb firm tofu
- 2 tablespoons reduced-sodium soy sauce
- 1½ cups basmati rice
- 1½ x 13-oz jars of chickpeas
- 1-inch piece of ginger
- 1 clove of garlic
- 1 grapefruit
- 1 orange
- 1 lime
- 1 tablespoon chili crisp
- 2 tablespoons runny honey
- 1 lb mixed green veg, such as green beans, broccolini, baby bok choy, asparagus

1 Light the grill (pages 16–19). Cut the tofu into 4 equal slices and, in a bowl, toss with 1 tablespoon of the soy. Let marinate for 20 minutes.

2 Add the rice and a pinch of sea salt to a cast-iron pan with 2 cups of boiling water and the chickpeas, juices and all. Cook on the medium zone with the grill lid on, vents open, for 15 minutes.

3 Meanwhile, to make a dressing, peel the ginger and garlic and finely grate into a bowl with half the grapefruit, orange and lime zest. Squeeze in the orange and lime juice, and mix with the chili crisp, honey and the remaining soy. Peel and segment or slice the grapefruit. Prep your chosen veg, trimming as appropriate, and halving the bok choy, if using.

4 Carefully remove the rice pan from the grill, cover it, and let steam while you cook the tofu and veg. Remove the tofu from the soy, pouring any excess into the dressing, spritz it with olive oil and season with black pepper. Cook on the hot zone for 5 minutes, or until marked, turning and moving to the medium zone if it's coloring too quickly – I like to brush it with a little of the dressing for the final minute. Cook the veg alongside, turning regularly until charred.

5 Plunge the tofu and veg straight into the remaining dressing. Divide the rice and chickpeas among serving bowls, then spoon on the veg, tofu, dressing and grapefruit segments.

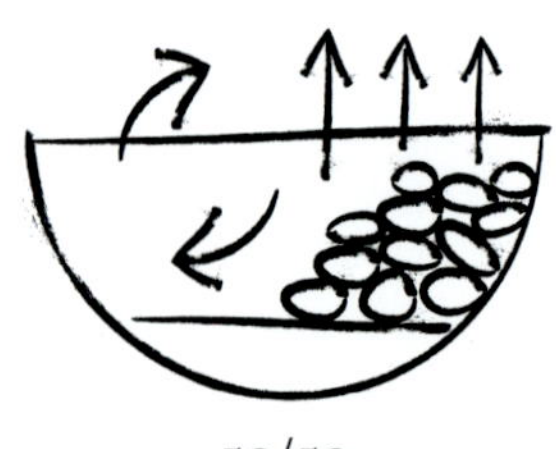

50/50

Sunshine stew & herb-stuffed sea bream

Serves 4 | 50 minutes

12 oz ripe tomatoes

8 oz new potatoes

2 small eggplants (8 oz each)

2 zucchini

2 red onions (12 oz total)

2 mixed-color bell peppers

6 sprigs of woody herbs, such as rosemary, thyme

3 cloves of garlic

1 cinnamon stick

1 teaspoon fennel seeds

1 tablespoon drained capers

6 green olives with pits

2 lemons

2 x 1-lb whole sea bream, branzino, or red snapper, scaled, gutted, fins removed

1 bunch of soft herbs (about 1 oz), such as Italian parsley, basil, mint, fennel fronds

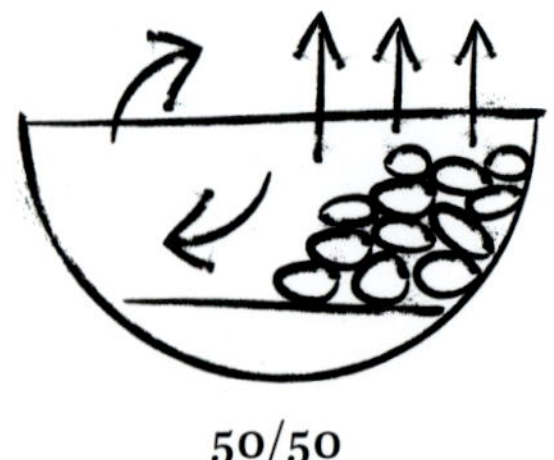

50/50

1 Light the grill (pages 16–19). Place the tomatoes and potatoes (halving any larger ones) on the medium zone. Halve the eggplants and zucchini lengthwise, peel and quarter the onions, tear open and seed the peppers, then grill it all for 20 minutes, or until charred and softened, turning regularly and transferring to a board once done.

2 Strip and chop the woody herb leaves. Peel and thinly slice the garlic. Add it all to a large shallow Dutch oven with the cinnamon, fennel seeds and capers. Pit and tear in the olives, use a vegetable peeler to strip in the lemon peel and add 4 tablespoons of olive oil.

3 When all the veg is off the grill, place the pan on the medium zone for 5 minutes, or until sizzling and the garlic is just starting to color. Meanwhile, scrape off any larger bits of blackened skin from the peppers, then roughly chop with the tomatoes, potatoes, eggplants, zucchini and onions. Scrape it all into the pan, add a splash of water, and cook for 10 minutes, stirring regularly. Carefully transfer the pan to the cool zone and let cook until soft and a pleasure to eat, while you prep and cook the fish.

4 Slice ½ a lemon and stuff into the fish cavities along with half the soft herbs. Generously season the fish with sea salt, then grill on the hot zone with the lid on, vents open, for 20 minutes, or until just cooked through – to check, go to the thickest part up near the head, and if the flesh is opaque and pulls easily away from the bone, it's done. Meanwhile, pound the remaining soft herbs in a mortar and pestle, muddle in 4 tablespoons of extra virgin olive oil and squeeze in the juice of 1 lemon, to taste.

5 Transfer the fish to a plate, let it cool a little, then use two forks to gently coax the fillets away from the fish, removing any bones as you go. Squeeze on the juice of ½ a lemon. Remove the cinnamon from the stew, season to perfection, and drizzle with a little extra virgin olive oil. Serve with the herb oil.

Chicken shawarma

Serves 4 | 1 hour 10 minutes, plus marinating

1¼ lbs boneless, skinless chicken thighs

2 heaping teaspoons baharat seasoning, plus extra to serve

2 cloves of garlic

2 lemons

1 red onion

2 heaping tablespoons Greek yogurt

1 x 15-oz can of pineapple rings in juice

4 flatbreads (or make your own, page 228)

½ a small head of red cabbage (about 10 oz)

½ a bunch of Italian parsley (about ½ oz)

12 oz ripe mixed-color tomatoes

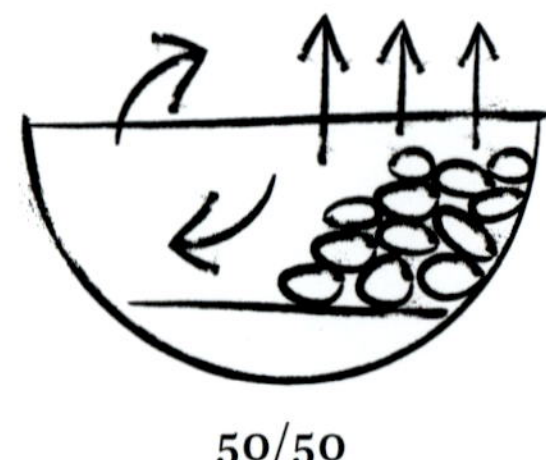

50/50

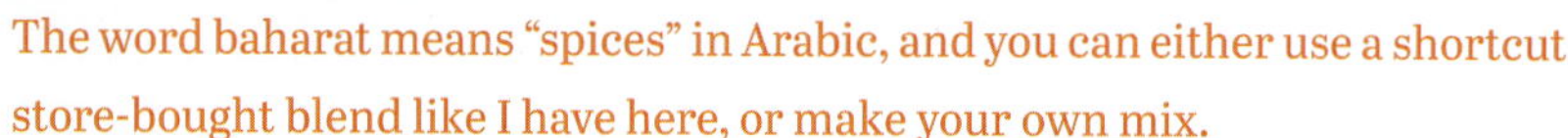

The word baharat means "spices" in Arabic, and you can either use a shortcut store-bought blend like I have here, or make your own mix.

1 Add the chicken to a bowl with the baharat and a pinch each of sea salt and black pepper. Peel and finely grate in the garlic and the zest of 1 lemon, then peel and quarter the onion and coarsely grate in one-quarter of it. Squeeze in the juice of the zested lemon, add the yogurt, then mix and massage it all into the chicken. You can cook it right away, but it's best left to marinate for up to 1 hour, or ideally overnight, in the fridge.

2 Light the grill (pages 16–19). Break the remaining onion quarters apart into petals. Drain the pineapple. Take your time threading the marinated chicken, onion petals and pineapple rings across 2 long metal skewers, alternating as you go, meaning you can cook and turn them as one (getting a friend to help you here will save time!). Spritz with olive oil.

3 Place on the hot zone for 5 minutes, turning with tongs to sear all over. Move to the cool zone to cook for 30 minutes with the lid on, vents open, turning every 10 minutes until cooked through. I like to prop it against a brick wrapped in foil so you can evenly color each of the four sides. Briefly warm the flatbreads alongside, or cook through, if making your own.

4 Use a vegetable peeler to shred the cabbage, or very thinly slice. Pick and sprinkle on the parsley, scrunch with the juice of the remaining lemon and season to perfection. Slice the tomatoes and sprinkle with a pinch of salt.

5 Slice between the skewers to help you portion up the chicken, then pile onto the flatbreads with some cabbage and tomatoes. I like to add a dollop of lemony yogurt and a drizzle of Chili sauce (page 204), and finish with an extra dusting of baharat. Serve the remaining cabbage and tomatoes on the side.

Skewer party

Chicken & chorizo skewers

Serves 4 | 25 minutes

1 red onion

2 mixed-color bell peppers

2 x 5-oz boneless, skinless chicken breasts

3 oz cured chorizo

1 heaping teaspoon Cajun seasoning

1 lime

1 tablespoon runny honey

1 Light the grill (pages 16–19). Peel and quarter the onion and break into petals. Chop the peppers into 1½-inch chunks. Use a sharp knife to carefully slice into the chicken breasts, then open each one out flat like a book and chop into scant 1-inch-thick chunks. Slice the chorizo into ¼-inch-thick rounds. Add it all to a large bowl with the Cajun seasoning, 1 tablespoon of olive oil and a pinch of black pepper and toss together.

2 Load everything up onto 4 long metal skewers, alternating as you go, and being mindful not to pack it on too tightly. Cook on the hot zone for 10 minutes, or until golden and cooked through, turning regularly, and moving the skewers to the medium or cooler zones if they're coloring too quickly. Remove and suspend over a serving bowl (like you see in the picture).

3 Squeeze on the lime juice, drizzle with the honey, then use a spoon to baste the skewers with the juices from the bottom of the bowl. Great served with Sriracha corn (page 94) and Charred flatbreads (page 228), with a simple slaw on the side, or as part of a bigger spread.

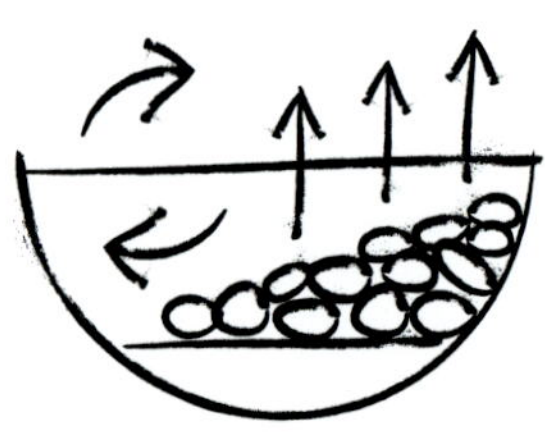

Graduated

Lamb kofta

Serves 4 | **35 minutes**

1 small red onion

1 lb ground lamb (20% fat)

1 teaspoon granulated garlic

1 tablespoon dried mint

1 teaspoon dried red chili flakes

1 teaspoon ground cumin

1 lemon

1 bunch of mixed soft herbs (about 1 oz), such as dill, mint, Italian parsley

⅔ cup Greek yogurt

½ an English cucumber (6 oz)

4 flatbreads (or make your own, page 228)

sumac, to serve

1 Peel and very thinly slice the onion, then add to a small bowl with 2 tablespoons of red wine vinegar and a good pinch of sea salt, scrunch together well, and let sit to quickly pickle.

2 Add the lamb to a bowl with the garlic, dried mint, chili flakes, cumin and a pinch each of salt and black pepper. Finely grate in the lemon zest, then get your clean hands in there and scrunch together well. Divide the mixture into four and, with wet hands, shape it around 4 metal skewers, using your hands to scrunch it on – a bit of texture is nice. Light the grill (pages 16–19).

3 Finely chop the herb leaves, reserving a few nice ones for garnish, then scrape into a bowl with the yogurt. Add 1 tablespoon of extra virgin olive oil and a squeeze of lemon juice, mix well, and season to perfection. Use a vegetable peeler to shave the cucumber into ribbons.

4 Cook the kofta on the hot zone for 25 minutes, or until charred and cooked through, turning regularly and moving to the medium or cool zone if coloring too quickly. Briefly warm the flatbreads or cook through, if making your own.

5 Spoon the herby yogurt onto the flatbreads, add the cucumber ribbons, place the kofta on top, drain and add the quick-pickled onions, and finish with a light dusting of sumac and the reserved herb leaves. Nice with Chili sauce (page 204) if you like an extra kick!

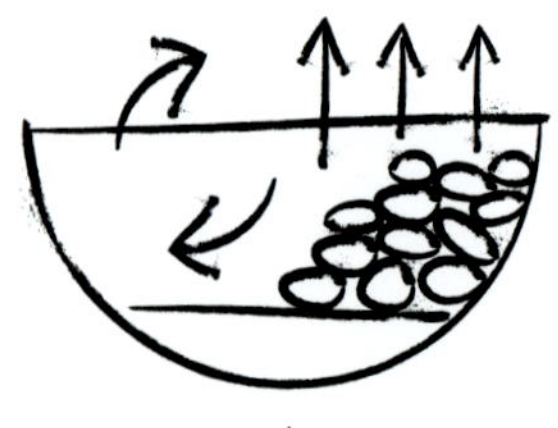

50/50

Halloumi & strawberry skewers

Serves 4 | 20 minutes

2 x 8-oz blocks of halloumi cheese

½ an English cucumber (6 oz)

12 ripe strawberries

1 lemon

1 bunch of mixed soft herbs (about 1 oz), such as basil, mint, Italian parsley

4 pitas

balsamic glaze, to serve

1 Light the grill (pages 16–19) and give the grate a really good brush to clean it – this will help prevent the skewers from sticking. Chop each block of halloumi into six. Halve the cucumber lengthwise, scrape out the seeds and chop into 8 pieces. Hull 8 strawberries. Gently skewer up the halloumi, cucumber and hulled strawberries across thin skewers, alternating as you go.

2 Finely grate the remaining 4 strawberries and lemon zest onto a platter. Squeeze on the lemon juice, add 1 tablespoon of extra virgin olive oil, mix together and season to perfection to make a dressing. Pick the herb leaves into a bowl, add a few drops of oil, and season.

3 Spritz the skewers with olive oil and cook on the hot zone for 5 minutes, or until golden and charred, turning with tongs and moving to the medium or cool zone if coloring too quickly. Lightly toast the pitas on the cool zone.

4 Place the skewers on the platter of dressing, and serve with the herb salad and toasted pitas for satisfying scooping or stuffing. Drizzle with a little of the balsamic glaze just before tucking in.

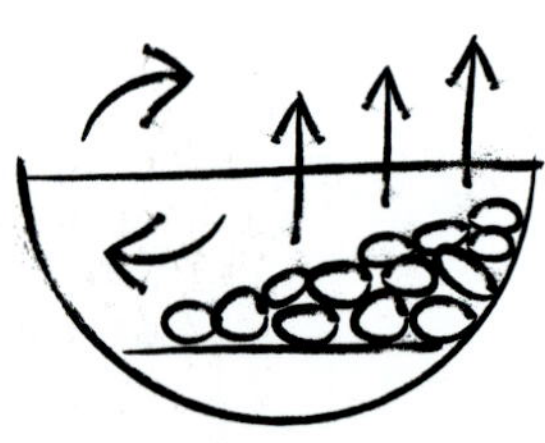

Graduated

Skewered sausages & creamy lentils

Serves 4 | **1 hour**

2 cloves of garlic

1 red onion

2 stalks of celery

1 lb rainbow chard

6 slices of bacon

½ a bunch of rosemary (about ⅓ oz)

1 heaping tablespoon tomato paste

2 x 15-oz cans of green lentils

½ x 16-oz jar of roasted red peppers

8 small pork sausages

1 cup heavy cream

your favorite mustard

1 Soak a handful of wood chips according to the package instructions, if you've got them. Light the grill (pages 16–19). Peel and thinly slice the garlic and onion, then trim the celery and thinly slice with the chard stems, reserving the leaves. Thinly slice the bacon.

2 Put a large shallow cast-iron pan on the hot zone, add the bacon and cook, stirring regularly until golden. Strip in the rosemary, add the garlic, onion, celery, chard stems and a very generous pinch of black pepper, and stir regularly until softened. Alongside, cook the chard leaves directly on the grill, moving frequently with tongs, and transferring to a board once wilted.

3 Stir the tomato paste into the pan, followed by the lentils, juices and all. Chop up and add the wilted chard. Drain the wood chips and place on the hot zone, if using. Put the grill lid on, vents open, and cook for 10 minutes.

4 Meanwhile, drain the peppers and cut lengthwise into strips the same width as your sausages. Skewer the sausages and peppers across 2 long metal skewers, alternating as you go, meaning you can cook and turn them as one.

5 Pour the cream into the lentil mixture. Place the sausage skewers on the medium-cool zone, cover again with the vents open, and cook for 20 minutes, or until the sausages are golden and cooked through, turning halfway and moving them to the hot zone if they need more color.

6 Mix up the creamy lentils, thinning with a splash of water, if needed, taste and tweak with a little mustard and red wine vinegar, then season to perfection with sea salt and pepper. Serve with the sausages and peppers, slicing down through the skewers before portioning.

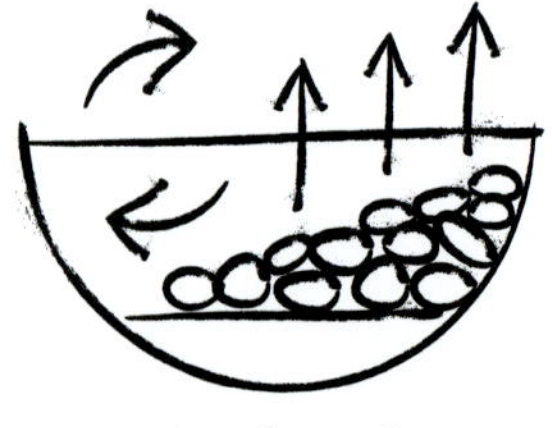

Graduated

Go veggie: Simply omit the bacon and swap in veggie sausages, adding 1 tablespoon of olive oil at the start of step 2.

Skewered sardines on toast

Serves 4 | 15 minutes

½ a clove of garlic

⅓ cup mayo (or make your own garlic mayo, page 210)

½ a bunch of Italian parsley (about ½ oz)

8 x 2-oz sardines, scaled, gutted, gills removed

4 slices of sourdough bread

1 lemon

1 Peel and finely grate the garlic, then mix into the mayo and season to perfection. Pick the parsley leaves and toss with 1 tablespoon of red wine vinegar and a pinch of sea salt.

2 Light the grill (pages 16–19) and give the grate a good brush – this will help prevent the sardines from sticking. Line up the sardines on a clean counter or board, alternating them head to tail. Carefully thread three skewers through them, so you can cook and turn them as one. Season with salt.

3 Grill on the hot zone for 2 to 3 minutes, or until beautifully charred, then turn for 1 minute on the other side, or until cooked through, moving to the medium or cool zone if they're coloring too quickly. Briefly toast the bread alongside, then line up on a board and drizzle with a little extra virgin olive oil.

4 Gently transfer the skewered sardines onto the toasts so they soak up all those lovely juices. Scatter on the dressed parsley, and serve with the garlic mayo and lemon wedges, for squeezing over.

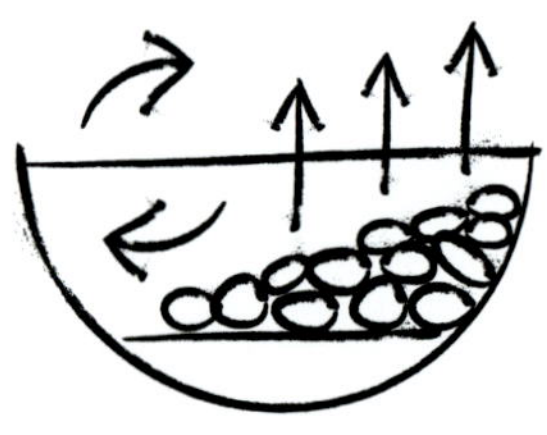

Graduated

Dr Loftus' lamb kebabs

Serves 4 | 30 minutes, plus marinating

2 lemons

1 heaping teaspoon grainy mustard

4 cloves of garlic

2 teaspoons each of dried thyme, dried oregano, dried basil

1 lb lamb neck fillet or leg of lamb

4 slices of bacon

1 onion

1 red bell pepper

4 oz chestnut or cremini mushrooms

½ a small zucchini

¾ cup ripe cherry tomatoes

This recipe is dedicated to my good friend and photographer of this book, David Loftus. This is the dish that his dear late mum used to make for him every Tuesday when she had the afternoon off work. It's simple, it's very delicious, and I hope it becomes a part of your family's recipe repertoire.

1 Finely grate the zest of 1 lemon into a large bowl and squeeze in the juice. Add the mustard, 2 tablespoons of red wine vinegar and 6 tablespoons of olive oil. Squash in the unpeeled garlic through a garlic press (or peel and finely grate it), then add all the dried herbs and season generously with sea salt and black pepper.

2 Trim any sinew off the lamb, then cut into generous 1-inch chunks. Slice the bacon a similar size. Peel the onion and cut the same size. Seed and chop the pepper, trim the mushrooms, halving any larger ones, and slice the zucchini into rounds. Add it all to the marinade with the tomatoes, mix well, then let sit for at least 30 minutes, or overnight in the fridge.

3 Light the grill (pages 16–19). Skewer everything onto metal skewers, alternating as you go. Cook the kebabs on the hot zone for 8 minutes, turning regularly to color all over, then transfer to the cool zone and cook lid on, vents open, for another 8 minutes, or until cooked through, turning occasionally.

4 Serve with lemon wedges, for squeezing over. Delicious with yogurt, salad and rice or flatbreads, or as part of a bigger spread.

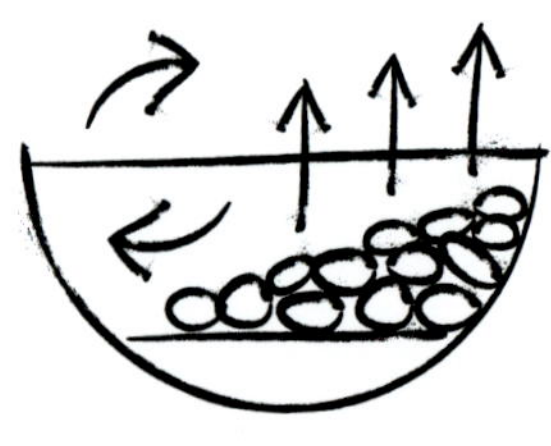

Graduated

Shrimp skewers & ajoblanco sauce

Serves 4 | **25 minutes**

16 raw shell-on jumbo shrimp

4 oz cured chorizo

2 lemons

16 padrón peppers or shishito peppers

2 cups slivered almonds

1 small clove of garlic

1 tablespoon sherry vinegar

½ a bunch of Italian parsley (about ½ oz)

1 pinch of smoked paprika, to serve

I've embraced some of the key ingredients of ajoblanco, a delicious cold Spanish soup, to create the perfect bed of sauce for these tasty shrimp skewers.

1 Peel the shrimp, leaving the tails on, then run a small sharp knife down the back of each, discarding the vein. Slice the chorizo into generous ¼-inch-thick rounds, halve and thinly slice 1 of the lemons, and prick the padrón peppers. Load everything up onto 4 long metal skewers, alternating as you go, and being mindful not to pack it all on too tightly.

2 Toast the almonds in a frying pan over a medium-high heat on the stove until lightly golden (or toast in a metal sieve over the hot zone, if you've got the grill lit already), then add them to a small blender or food processor. Peel and add the garlic, along with the sherry vinegar and 1 cup of cold water. Season with sea salt and blitz until you have a thick, smooth paste, thinning with extra splashes of cold water, if needed. Spread onto a serving platter.

3 Pound the parsley, stems and all, with a pinch of salt in a mortar and pestle to a fine paste, then finely grate in the zest of the remaining lemon and muddle in 4 tablespoons of extra virgin olive oil.

4 Light the grill (pages 16–19). Cook the skewers on the hot zone for 3 to 4 minutes, or until beautifully charred and cooked through, turning regularly and moving to the medium or cool zone if they're coloring too quickly. Transfer to the serving platter, drizzle with some parsley oil, squeeze on the remaining lemon juice and finish with a nice dusting of paprika.

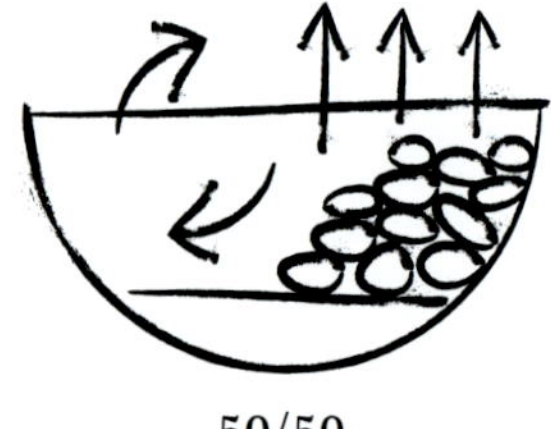

50/50

Blushing bavette skewers & ssamjang

Serves 4 | 15 minutes, plus marinating

- 2 teaspoons reduced-sodium soy sauce
- 1 teaspoon toasted sesame oil
- 1 tablespoon runny honey
- 1 clove of garlic
- 1 lb bavette steak (sometimes labeled flap meat)
- 1 head of iceberg lettuce
- 1 lb mixed crunchy veg, such as radishes, English cucumber, carrot, green cabbage
- 1 lime
- 2 heaping tablespoons ssamjang

Ssamjang is a popular Korean paste or sauce that brings big, bold flavor to all sorts of dishes, pairing particularly well with this blushing bavette.

1. Mix the soy, sesame oil and honey in a large bowl. Peel and finely grate in the garlic and add 1 teaspoon of black pepper. Cut the beef into generous 1-inch chunks, then add to the bowl, mix and let marinate for at least 30 minutes, or overnight in the fridge. Light the grill (pages 16–19).

2. Skewer up the marinated beef, being mindful not to pack it on too tightly, and cook on the hot zone for 8 minutes for blushing, or until cooked to your liking, turning with tongs to ensure even cooking.

3. Meanwhile, separate out the lettuce into cups, then prep, shred, thinly slice or matchstick the mixed crunchy veg to your liking and pile onto a platter. Cut the lime into wedges.

4. Serve the skewers with the crunchy veg and ssamjang, stuffing it all into the iceberg cups before tucking in. I like to spoon on some of the tasty resting juices, and add a squeeze of lime, to taste. Outrageously good!

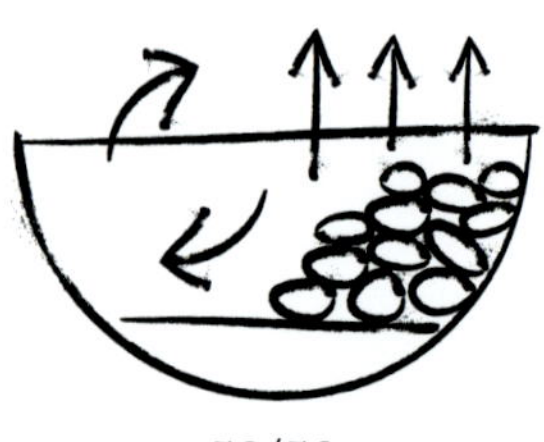

50/50

Sticky sriracha tofu

Serves 2 | 25 minutes

2 nests of instant vermicelli rice noodles (3 oz total)

½ a bunch of cilantro (about ½ oz)

½ an English cucumber (6 oz)

8 oz radishes

1 tablespoon rice wine vinegar

1-inch piece of ginger

2 tablespoons reduced-sodium soy sauce

12 oz firm tofu

6 oz shiitake mushrooms

3 tablespoons sriracha sauce

2 tablespoons runny honey

3 tablespoons unsalted roasted peanuts

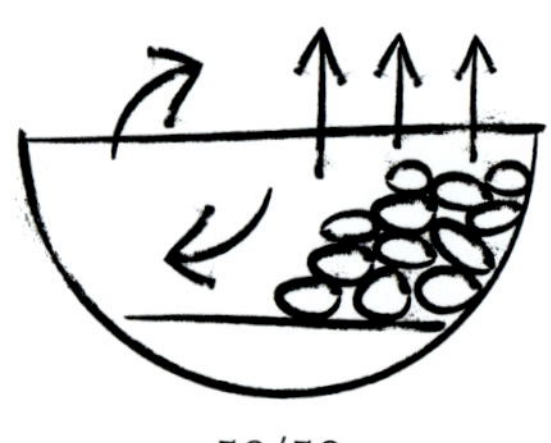

50/50

1 Soak a handful of wood chips according to the package instructions. Put the noodles into a bowl, just cover with boiling water and let sit to rehydrate for a few minutes, then drain and set aside. Pick the cilantro.

2 Use a vegetable peeler to shave the cucumber into ribbons. Very thinly slice half the radishes. Toss both with the rice wine vinegar and a small pinch of sea salt in a large serving bowl. If using wooden skewers, soak them now. Light the grill (pages 16–19).

3 Peel and finely grate the ginger into another bowl, then mix in the soy and 1 tablespoon of olive oil. Chop the tofu into generous 1-inch chunks, halve the remaining radishes and add to the bowl along with the mushrooms. Toss to coat, then thread onto skewers, alternating as you go.

4 Drain the wood chips and place on the hot zone. Cook the skewers on the medium zone, lid on, vents open, for 10 minutes, or until cooked through, turning regularly. Mix the sriracha with the honey and brush over the skewers, cooking for a couple more minutes, or until sticky and beautifully charred. Toast the nuts in a metal sieve alongside, removing once golden, then toss the nuts in the remaining sriracha and honey mixture.

5 Gently toss the noodles and cilantro leaves with the cucumber and radishes, then scatter on the sticky peanuts. Serve with the tofu skewers.

Peanutty chicken skewers

Serves 4–8 as part of a spread | 25 minutes, plus marinating

1 tablespoon ground coriander

1 teaspoon ground cumin

½ teaspoon ground turmeric

2 limes

⅔ cup unsweetened coconut cream

1½ lbs chicken tenders

1 cup unsalted roasted peanuts

2 tablespoons Thai red curry paste

1 teaspoon reduced-sodium soy sauce

½ a bunch of cilantro (about ½ oz)

1 fresh red chili

1 Add the ground coriander, cumin and turmeric to a large bowl. Finely grate in the zest of 1 lime and squeeze in the juice. Add 1 tablespoon of olive oil, 2 tablespoons of coconut cream and a pinch each of sea salt and black pepper. Mix with the chicken and let marinate for at least 20 minutes. If using wooden skewers, soak them now. Light the grill (pages 16–19).

2 Thread one piece of chicken onto each skewer. Pound the peanuts in a mortar and pestle until fine, then add half to a small cast-iron or enamel pan. Whisk the Thai red curry paste with the remaining coconut cream, add to the pan, and place on the cool zone for 5 minutes, or until bubbling and reduced. Add the soy and squeeze in lime juice to taste, thinning to a saucy consistency with a splash of water, if needed.

3 Line up the skewers on the hot zone (keeping the ends of the skewers away from direct heat) and cook lid on, vents open, for 7 to 10 minutes, or until charred and cooked through, flipping halfway and spritzing occasionally with olive oil, moving to the cooler zone if they're coloring too quickly.

4 Squeeze on the remaining lime juice, to taste, tear on the cilantro leaves, then thinly slice and scatter on the chili. To serve, take a skewer, dunk it in the sauce, then dip it in the crushed nuts – delicious.

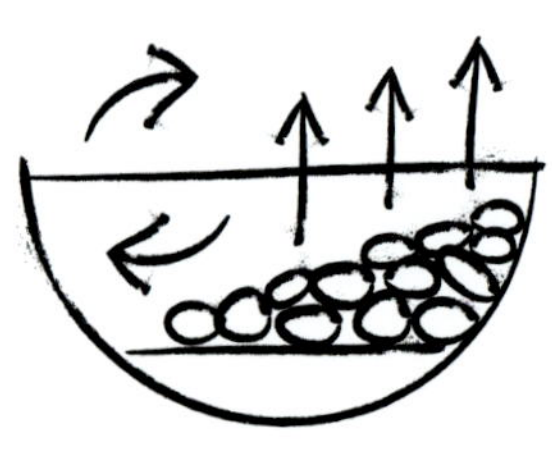

Graduated

Spiced pork kebabs

Serves 4 | 30 minutes, plus marinating

4 tablespoons madras curry paste

1 lb pork tenderloin

12 oz baby new potatoes

1 red onion

3 fresh green chilies

½ a bunch of mixed soft herbs (about ½ oz), such as mint, cilantro

1 In a bowl, thin the curry paste with 2 tablespoons of red wine vinegar. Trim any sinew off the pork, cut into generous 1-inch chunks, toss into the bowl, cover, and let marinate for at least 30 minutes, or overnight in the fridge.

2 Cook the potatoes in a small pan of boiling salted water on the stove for 15 minutes, or until tender, then drain and cut in half.

3 Light the grill (pages 16–19). Cut the onion into six wedges, leaving the root ends attached, then separate into pairs of petals. Halve and seed the chilies, then halve again. Divide it all among 4 long metal skewers alternating with the marinated pork and potatoes, then spritz with olive oil.

4 Sear on the hot zone, lid on, vents open, for 7 minutes to get a nice color, turning regularly, then move to the medium-cool zone, lid on, vents open, for another 7 minutes, or until cooked through, turning halfway.

5 Pick and sprinkle on the soft herbs to serve. Great with fluffy rice, cooling yogurt and a nice stack of pappadams.

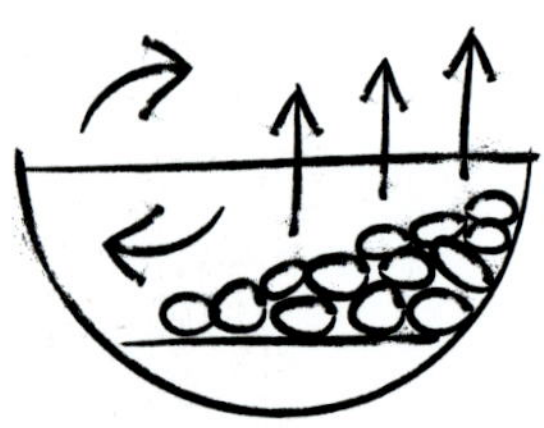

Graduated

Spiced chicken kebabs & butter sauce

Serves 4–6 | 1 hour 15 minutes

- 1-inch piece of ginger
- 1 clove of garlic
- 1 lemon
- 1 teaspoon each chili powder and ground cumin
- ½ teaspoon each ground coriander and ground turmeric
- ¼ cup plain yogurt
- 2 x 5-oz boneless, skinless chicken breasts
- 1 lb boneless, skinless chicken thighs
- ½ a ripe pineapple
- 2 small red onions
- 1 fresh red chili
- 1½ lbs ripe tomatoes
- ⅓ cup unsalted cashews
- ¼ teaspoon ground fenugreek
- 2 tablespoons unsalted butter
- ⅔ cup heavy cream

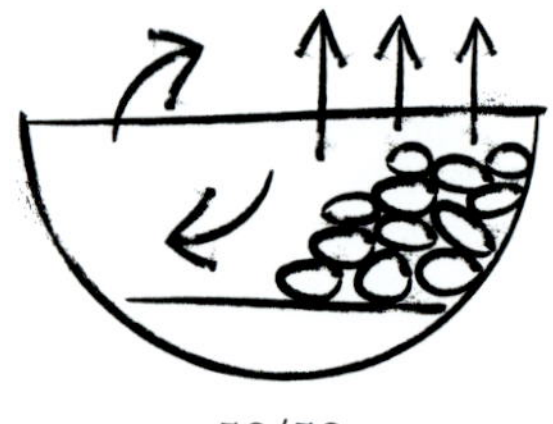

50/50

Inspired by the incredible flavors of butter chicken, here I'm serving up grilled tandoori-style kebabs with a flavor-packed sauce, fit for a feast.

1 Peel the ginger and garlic and finely grate into a large bowl with the zest of ½ a lemon, squeeze in the juice of that half, then add ½ teaspoon each of the chili powder and cumin, along with the ground coriander, turmeric, yogurt and a pinch each of sea salt and black pepper. Mix together. Cut the chicken breasts into 2-inch chunks and add to the bowl along with the thighs. Toss to coat, keeping the breast meat and thighs separate. You can cook right away, or let marinate for up to 1 hour in the fridge.

2 Light the grill (pages 16–19). Peel the pineapple and halve lengthwise, discarding the core. Chop into 1½-inch chunks, toss with the marinated chicken breasts, then thread both onto large metal skewers. Peel and halve the onions, cut one half into quarters and break into petals, then thread onto another large metal skewer along with the chicken thighs.

3 For the butter sauce, cut the remaining onions into thick slices, then place on the hot zone. Prick and add the chili and tomatoes, char it all for 10 minutes, turning regularly, then transfer to a board.

4 Put a shallow Dutch oven on the hot zone and add 1 tablespoon of olive oil, the cashews, the remaining ½ teaspoon each of chili powder and cumin, the fenugreek and the butter. Pinch off and discard the charred tomato skins, halve and seed the chili, then add to the pan along with the onion rounds, busting up the tomatoes as you go. Season with salt and pepper, carefully transfer to the cool zone to simmer for 15 minutes, or until saucy, then pour in the cream, letting it all mingle together nicely. Remove from the grill.

5 Place the thigh skewer on the hot zone with the lid on, vents open, for 5 minutes, then add the breast skewers and cook for 10 to 15 minutes, or until cooked through, turning halfway, spritzing with oil and moving to the cooler zones if coloring too quickly. Remove and squeeze on the remaining lemon juice, then serve. Great with fresh cilantro, my Coconut & cilantro flat-bread (page 84), a lemony crunchy veg salad, and mango chutney.

Coconut & cilantro flatbread

Serves 4–6 | 10 minutes, plus resting

Add **1¾ cups of self-rising flour** to a large bowl with a pinch of sea salt and **½ x 14-oz can of coconut milk**. Finely grate in the zest of **½ a lemon**, squeeze in the juice, then mix until it comes together. Pick and finely chop the leaves from **½ a bunch of cilantro (about ½ oz)**, then use your fingertips to mix into the dough until combined, adding a little extra flour, if needed. Knead briefly on a lightly floured surface until you have a soft dough, then oil, cover and let rest for 15 minutes. Use clean oiled hands to pull, stretch and flatten the dough to a scant ½ inch thick. Grill on the medium zone for 4 to 5 minutes, or until charred, puffed up and cooked through, flipping halfway and rubbing with **1 tablespoon of softened unsalted butter**, and moving to cooler areas of the grill as needed.

Note: If you can't find self-rising flour, use an equal volume of all-purpose flour plus 1½ teaspoons of baking powder and a pinch of salt for each cup of flour.

Salads with attitude & veg galore

Charred radicchio, orange & burrata salad

Serves 2 as a main / 4 as a side | 20 minutes

2 tablespoons runny honey

2 clementines or small oranges

2 heads of radicchio or Treviso or 4 red endives

2 heads of lettuce, such as Bibb, Boston, gem

scant ½ cup blanched hazelnuts

1 bunch of thyme or rosemary (about ⅔ oz)

1 x 6-oz ball of burrata or buffalo mozzarella cheese

1 Light the grill (pages 16–19). Mix 1 tablespoon each of honey and red wine vinegar and 2 tablespoons of extra virgin olive oil in a large shallow serving bowl, and season to perfection. Peel 1 of the clementines and thinly slice into rounds, then halve the other. Trim and thinly slice the bottom 1½ inches of each radicchio, then separate the leaves. Separate out the lettuce leaves.

2 Char the halved clementine, cut side down, until nicely marked, then use tongs to squeeze the juice into the bowl of dressing.

3 Put a small cast-iron pan on the grill and toast the nuts for a few minutes, tossing regularly and removing once golden. Scatter the radicchio and lettuce leaves onto the grill alongside, turning with tongs until beautifully charred and transferring to the bowl of dressing as they're done.

4 Spritz the bunch of herbs with a little olive oil, then grill for 30 seconds, turning halfway so it doesn't scorch. As soon as they're cool enough to handle, strip the leaves into the salad, then toss and scrunch it all together.

5 Add the sliced clementine, sliced radicchio, chop and add the toasted nuts, tear in the burrata, drizzle with the remaining tablespoon of honey, and serve. Great as it is, with hunks of crusty bread, or as part of a bigger spread.

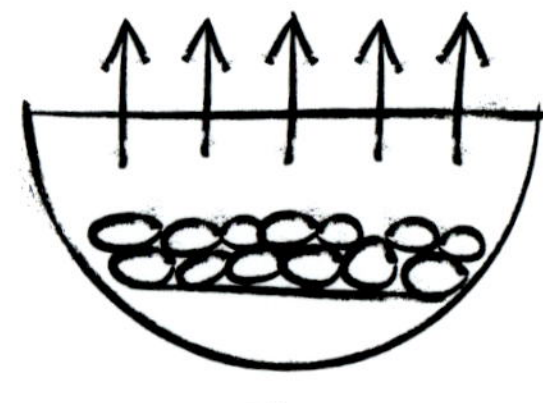

Flat

ASHDON
Honey

Grilled caponata

Serves 4 as a main / 8 as a side | 40 minutes

2 small eggplants (8 oz each)

1 head of celery

2 red onions (12 oz total)

1 lemon

1¼ lbs ripe mixed-color tomatoes

2 cloves of garlic

1 cinnamon stick

⅓ cup pine nuts

1 heaping tablespoon drained capers

12 pitted green olives

1 teaspoon dried oregano

1 bunch of Italian parsley (about 1 oz)

1 orange

1 Light the grill (pages 16–19). Slice the eggplants lengthwise a scant ½ inch thick. Remove the outer celery stalks and save for another day, then halve the celery heart lengthwise. Peel and halve the onions. Halve the lemon. Put it all on the hot zone with the whole tomatoes and grill for 10 to 12 minutes, turning regularly, transferring to your board when nicely marked and moving to the medium or cooler zones if coloring too quickly.

2 Add 2 tablespoons of olive oil to a large shallow cast-iron pan. Peel, thinly slice and add the garlic, along with the cinnamon, pine nuts, capers, olives and oregano. Place on the hot zone to fry and sizzle for 5 minutes, stirring regularly, while you chop the onion, celery and eggplants into scant 1-inch chunks.

3 Stir the chopped veg into the pan, then spend a moment pinching the skins off the tomatoes. Mash the tomatoes into the mix, then use tongs to squeeze in the grilled lemon juice (discarding any seeds). Simmer for 15 to 20 minutes on the medium zone with the lid on, vents open, or until the veg are soft, then carefully remove the pan from the grill.

4 Pick and chop the parsley, stir into the pan, season to perfection, then finely grate in the orange zest and squeeze in the juice. Finish with a drizzle of extra virgin olive oil, if you like. Great as part of a bigger spread, and a perfect treat served with grilled toasts and torn mozzarella, like you see here.

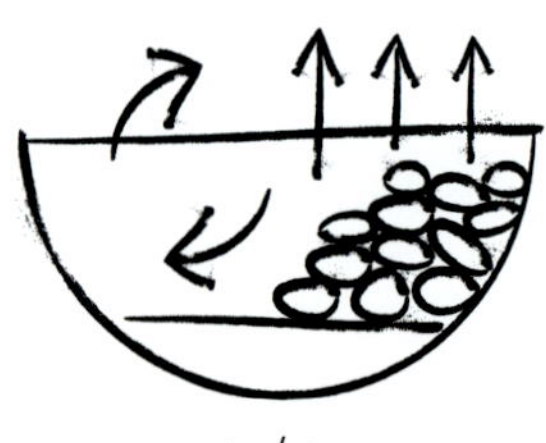

50/50

Med-style greens

Serves 4 | 15 minutes

½ a lemon

4 sun-dried tomatoes in oil

12 mixed-color olives, with pits

1 tablespoon drained capers

1 lb rainbow chard

2 sprigs of basil

1 Light the grill (pages 16–19). Squeeze the lemon juice into a large shallow bowl and add 1 tablespoon of red wine vinegar and 2 tablespoons of extra virgin olive oil. Finely chop and add the sun-dried tomatoes, tear in the olives, discarding the pits, add the capers, mix, and season to perfection.

2 Strip the chard leaves from the stems, leaving the stems whole but trimming away any sad ends. Give it all a wash and gently shake dry, leaving some residual moisture on the leaves. Grill the stems on the medium zone for 2 to 3 minutes, or until lightly charred, then add the leaves for another 2 to 3 minutes, letting them wilt and steam, moving regularly with tongs.

3 Transfer it all to your board as it's done, then roughly chop and toss with the dressing. Tear in the basil leaves and serve. Delicious as part of a bigger spread, or with Arrabiatta chicken drumsticks (page 140).

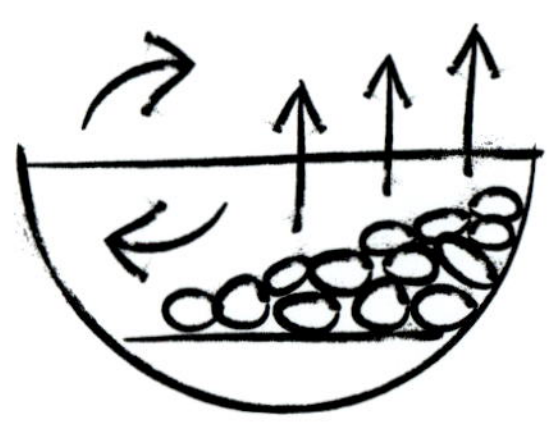

Graduated

Sriracha corn

Serves 4–6 | 15 minutes

4 ears of corn, husked

2 tablespoons mayo (or make your own, page 210)

1 tablespoon sriracha sauce

1 to 2 limes

2 scallions

1 Light the grill (pages 16–19). Place the corn on the hot zone for 10 minutes, or until softened and nicely charred, using tongs to roll the ears back and forth to the medium and cool zones as needed so you can control how quickly they color, then transfer to a board.

2 Mix the mayo and sriracha, then finely grate in the zest of 1 lime and squeeze in the juice to make a dressing. Trim and thinly slice the scallions.

3 Slice the corn off the cobs and mix with the dressing. Season to perfection, tweak with more lime juice if needed, then scatter on the scallions. Great as part of a bigger spread, paired with a grilled steak, or with my Chicken & chorizo skewers (page 60) or Paprika pulled pork (page 178).

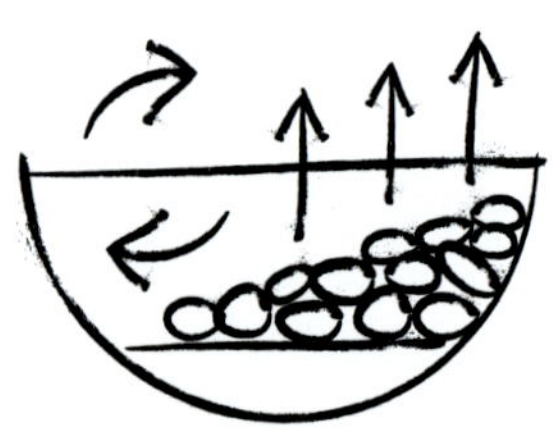

Graduated

Grilled green grain salad

Serves 6–8 as a side | 25 minutes

1 lb mixed asparagus, broccolini & green beans

1 bunch of scallions

2 fresh green chilies

2 x 8.5-oz packages of cooked mixed grains

½ a bunch of mint (about ½ oz)

½ a bunch of Italian parsley (about ½ oz)

1 large ripe avocado

1 lemon

2 oz feta cheese

2 tablespoons pumpkin seeds

1 Light the grill (pages 16–19). Trim the asparagus, broccolini, green beans and scallions, then spritz with olive oil. Prick the chilies. Working in batches, if needed, line up the veg in a grill basket for easier handling, and grill for 6 minutes, or until softened, turning halfway and charring the chilies alongside. Transfer it all to your board.

2 Heat the grains according to the package instructions, then add to a large serving bowl. Finely chop the charred veg, leaving the asparagus and broccolini tips whole, and scrape into the bowl.

3 To make a dressing, pick most of the mint into a blender, reserving the nice baby leaves. Add the parsley, stems and all, then halve, pit and scoop in the avocado. Scrape off the bigger bits of blackened skin from the chilies and seed, then add to the blender along with the lemon juice and 2 tablespoons of extra virgin olive oil. Blitz until smooth, thinning with splashes of water until you have a drizzleable consistency. Season to perfection.

4 Pour the dressing over the salad, gently toss to coat, then crumble in the feta, and sprinkle on the pumpkin seeds and reserved mint leaves. Delicious as it is, as part of a bigger spread, or paired with my Pomegranate & harissa chicken (page 156) or Quick beet mackerel (page 32).

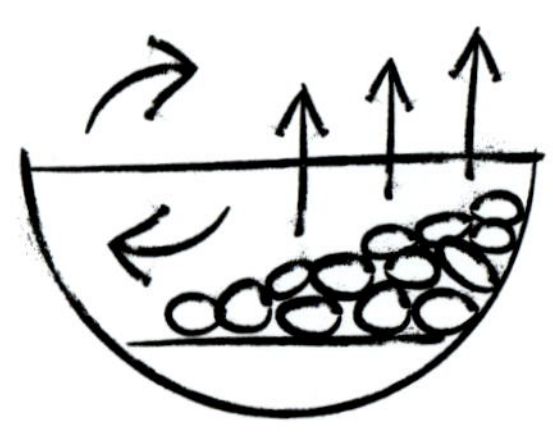

Graduated

Pickle potato salad

Serves 4–6 as a side | 30 minutes

1 small red onion

½ cup sour cream

½ cup Greek yogurt

1 bunch of dill (about ⅔ oz)

8 cornichons

½ a lemon

2 oz feta cheese

2 lbs baby new potatoes

1 Peel and very thinly slice the onion, add to a small bowl with 3 tablespoons of red wine vinegar and a good pinch of sea salt, scrunch together well, and let sit to quickly pickle.

2 In a nice serving bowl, mix the sour cream and yogurt together. Finely chop the dill and cornichons and scrape into the bowl with a splash of juice from the cornichon jar. Finely grate in the lemon zest, squeeze in the juice, crumble in the feta, add 1 tablespoon of extra virgin olive oil, mix well and season to perfection. Light the grill (pages 16–19).

3 Ideally you want all your potatoes to be a similar size, so halve any larger ones. Grill on the hot zone for 5 minutes, turning regularly until charred, then move to the medium zone with the lid on, vents open, for 15 minutes, or until cooked through. As they're done, lightly squash them, add straight into the bowl of dressing and toss well to coat.

4 Drain the quick-pickled onions and pile on top, then serve. Great warm, at room temperature or cold, and the perfect addition to any cookout spread. It's particularly delicious with my Paprika pulled pork (page 178), Ultimate pork ribs (page 158) or Quick beet mackerel (page 32).

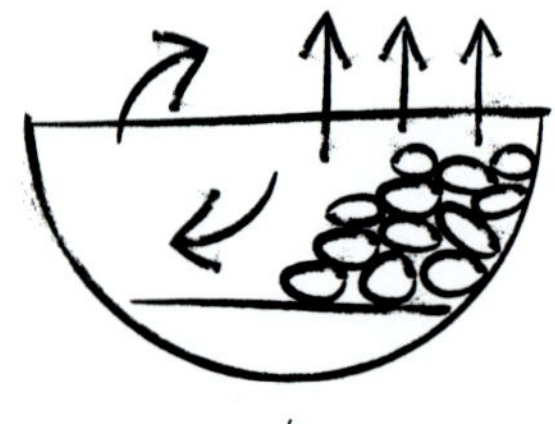

50/50

Herby grilled carrots & feta

Serves 4 | 35 minutes

1½ lbs mixed-color carrots

2 clementines

1 tablespoon runny honey

2 tablespoons mixed seeds, such as pumpkin, sunflower, flax

½ a bunch of Italian parsley (about ½ oz)

4 oz feta cheese

1 Light the grill (pages 16–19). Wash the carrots and gently shake dry, retaining some residual moisture, then halve or quarter any larger ones lengthwise. Halve the clementines. Place it all on the hot zone, clementines cut side down, and cook for 10 minutes with the lid on, vents open, or until nicely charred, turning regularly with tongs.

2 Transfer the charred clementines to your board, and move the carrots to the cool zone to cook for another 20 minutes, lid on, vents open, or until tender.

3 Add 2 tablespoons each of red wine vinegar and extra virgin olive oil to a large shallow bowl. Use tongs to squeeze in the juice from the charred clementine halves, add the honey, seeds, and a pinch each of sea salt and black pepper, and mix well. Pick and finely chop the parsley leaves.

4 Transfer the cooked carrots straight into the bowl of dressing, add the chopped parsley and toss well, then break in the feta and gently toss again. Delicious dished up as it is, served simply with grilled meat or grains, or alongside my Classic leg of lamb (page 144).

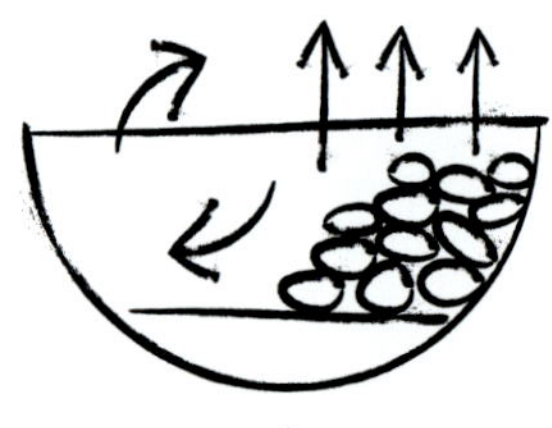

50/50

Squash, sage & rice salad

Serves 4–6 as a side | 1 hour 10 minutes

1 butternut squash (2½ lbs)

1½ cups basmati rice

½ cup sliced almonds

1 bunch of sage (about ⅔ oz)

½ cup dried cranberries

1 lemon

If you're grilling other things, this is a great one to do alongside, as you can simply leave the whole squash underneath the grill doing its thing, hands-off, then assemble this beautiful and ever-so-delicious salad to serve.

1 Light the grill (pages 16–19). Nestle the squash next to the hot coals and let it blacken and soften for 1 hour, or until tender. Carefully remove with tongs.

2 When the squash is nearly done, add the rice and a pinch of sea salt to a saucepan with 2½ cups of boiling water. Cover and cook over medium heat on the stove for 12 minutes, or until the rice is tender and the water has been absorbed. (Alternatively, cook the rice in a cast-iron pan on the medium zone of the grill, with the lid on, vents open, for 15 minutes, then remove and let the rice steam with the lid on for 5 minutes.)

3 Toast the almonds in a frying pan on the stove, or in a cast-iron pan on the grill, moving regularly until lightly golden, then remove, leaving the pan on the heat. Add ¼ cup of olive oil, pick in the sage leaves and fry until crispy, then transfer to paper towels, reserving the oil.

4 Halve the squash lengthwise and scrape out the seeds, then use a spoon to scoop all the soft flesh into a large shallow bowl, discarding the seeds and blackened skin. Add the rice, toasted almonds, crispy sage, reserved oil and dried cranberries. Finely grate in the lemon zest and squeeze in the juice, toss really well until the rice turns a beautiful orange hue and the sage is broken up, then season to perfection. Perfect as part of a bigger spread, and delicious alongside everything from simple steak to Med-style greens (page 92) or Herby grilled carrots & feta (page 100).

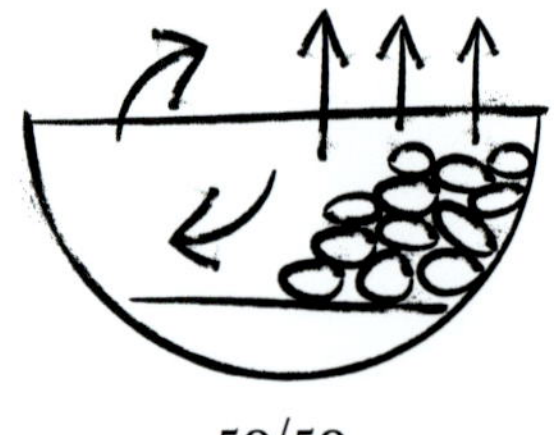

50/50

Zucchini & ricotta salad

Serves 2 as a main / 4 as a side | 25 minutes

2 large ripe tomatoes

2 tablespoons shelled unsalted pistachios

⅔ cup ricotta cheese

1 lemon

1 lb baby zucchini

2 sprigs of basil

Singing of summer, this is one of those beautiful dishes that's at its best when made with bang-in-season zucchini and tomatoes. An utter joy.

1 Light the grill (pages 16–19). Grill the tomatoes whole on the hot zone, lid on, vents open, for 10 minutes, or until blackened and softened. Meanwhile, crush the pistachios in a mortar and pestle or finely chop. Beat the ricotta with half the lemon juice, season to perfection and spread onto a serving platter.

2 Transfer the tomatoes to your board and add the zucchini to the hot zone, halving any larger ones lengthwise. Grill for 12 minutes, or until softened and nicely marked, turning regularly with tongs.

3 Meanwhile, scrape off and discard the bigger bits of blackened skin from the tomatoes. Quarter them and remove the core, then, in a shallow bowl, mash them up with a fork. Squeeze in the remaining lemon juice, add 1 tablespoon of extra virgin olive oil, and season to perfection.

4 Transfer the cooked zucchini straight into the tomato dressing and toss well. Pile them on top of the ricotta, spooning on any excess dressing. Sprinkle with the nuts, tear on the basil leaves, and serve. Great as it is, alongside my Classic leg of lamb (page 144), or as part of a bigger spread.

Easy swap: Feel free to use regular zucchini instead – simply quarter them lengthwise before cooking.

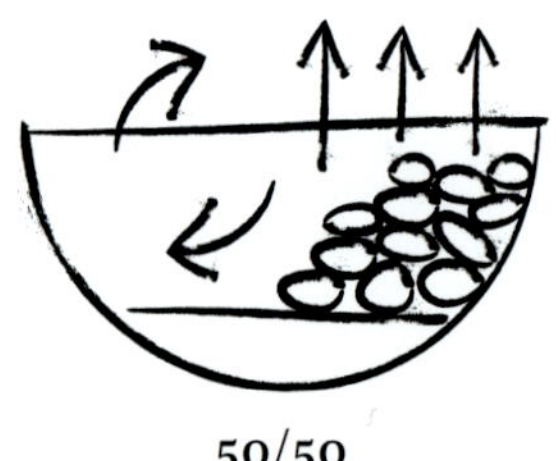

50/50

Yogurt pasta salad

Serves 8–10 as a side | 15 minutes

1 lb dried pasta, such as elbow macaroni, farfalle, shells, fusilli

2¼ cups Greek yogurt

1 heaping teaspoon dried mint

½ a clove of garlic

1 lemon

scant ½ cup blanched hazelnuts

1 heaping teaspoon fennel seeds

1 pinch of dried red chili flakes

⅓ cup pine nuts

You get a wonderful contrast between cool dressed pasta and sizzling hot nuts in this take on macarona bil laban, a pasta dish with yogurt sauce popular in several Levantine countries. It's a brilliant addition to any spread.

1. Cook the pasta in a large pot of boiling salted water on the stove according to the package instructions. Drain, transfer to a large shallow serving bowl and toss with 1 tablespoon of extra virgin olive oil. Light the grill (pages 16–19).

2. Add the yogurt and dried mint to the pasta. Peel and finely grate in the garlic. Finely grate the lemon zest into a small cast-iron pan, then squeeze the juice over the pasta. Mix well, and season to perfection.

3. Add the hazelnuts, fennel seeds, chili flakes and 1 tablespoon of olive oil to the pan of lemon zest, and place on the grill, stirring regularly until lightly golden. Add the pine nuts and fry until everything is dark golden and sizzling, then pour straight over the pasta, and serve.

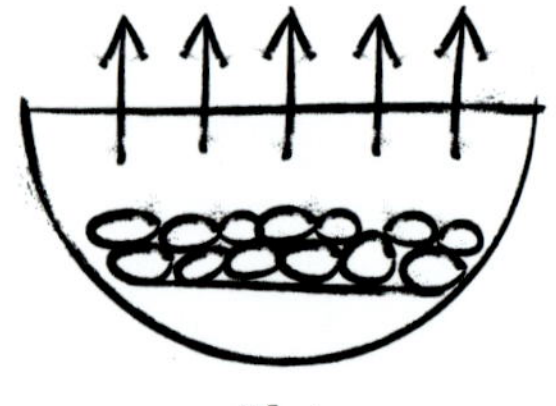

Flat

Best-ever tomato salad

Serves 6 as a side | 25 minutes

2¼ lbs ripe mixed-color tomatoes

1 clove of garlic

½ tablespoon balsamic glaze, plus extra to serve

1 x 4-oz ball of mozzarella cheese

2 sprigs of basil

1 Light the grill (pages 16–19). Soak a handful of wood chips according to the package instructions.

2 Take the larger tomatoes (about 8 oz in total) and place on the hot zone. Put the drained wood chips alongside to impart a lovely smoky flavor. Cook with the lid on, vents open, for 10 minutes, or until the tomatoes are blackened and blistered all over. Remove and let sit until cool enough to handle.

3 Pinch off and discard the blackened tomato skins, adding the soft insides to a blender. Peel and finely grate in the garlic. Add the balsamic glaze and 1 tablespoon of extra virgin olive oil, then blitz until smooth and season to perfection with sea salt and black pepper.

4 Chop or slice the remaining fresh tomatoes, leaving any small cherry ones whole, and toss with the dressing in a nice shallow serving bowl. Tear on the mozzarella, season it, pick and sprinkle on the basil and finish with an extra drizzle of balsamic glaze and a few drops of extra virgin olive oil, if you like.

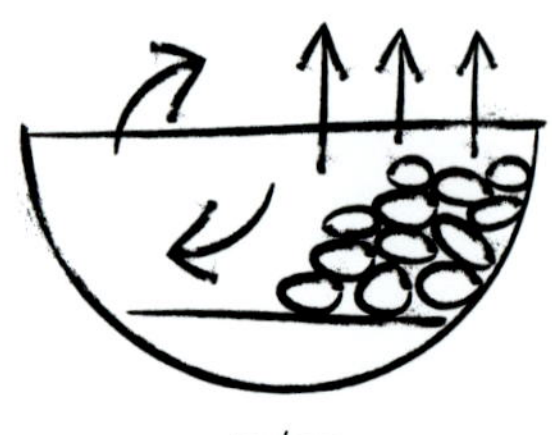

50/50

Charred squash & tahini chickpea salad

Serves 4 as a main / 8 as a side | 50 minutes

1 butternut squash (2½ lbs)

2 tablespoons tahini

1 clementine or small orange

½ a lemon

1½ x 13-oz jars of chickpeas

1 bunch of mixed soft herbs (about 1 oz), such as Italian parsley, basil, mint

1 tablespoon dukkah

¼ cup smoked almonds

1 pomegranate

½ cup labneh or thick Greek yogurt

1 Light the grill (pages 16–19). Carefully cut the squash into quarters lengthwise, then place on the medium zone and cook with the lid on, vents open, for 45 minutes, or until soft and charred, turning occasionally and moving to the cooler zone if coloring too quickly.

2 Meanwhile, put 1 tablespoon of tahini into a large shallow serving bowl, squeeze in the clementine and lemon juice, add 1 tablespoon each of red wine vinegar and extra virgin olive oil and mix well. Drain and stir in the chickpeas, pick, roughly chop and add most of the herb leaves, reserving a few nice ones for garnish, and the dukkah. Finely chop the almonds.

3 Transfer the charred squash to your board, scrape out and discard the seeds, peel, if you like, then slice a scant ½ inch thick and toss with the tahini chickpeas. Season to perfection. Halve the pomegranate and, holding one half cut side down in your palm, bash the back with a spoon so the seeds tumble out over the salad. Gently toss together. Dollop on the labneh, drizzle with the remaining tahini,and sprinkle with the chopped almonds and reserved herb leaves. Serve, adding extra pomegranate seeds and a drizzle of extra virgin olive oil, if you like.

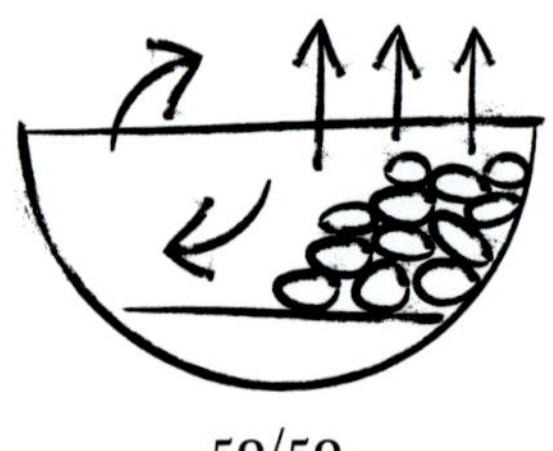

50/50

Beautiful Georgian-style stuffed eggplant

Serves 4–8 as part of a spread | 35 minutes

2 eggplants (about 14 oz each)

1 cup shelled walnut halves

½ a clove of garlic

½ teaspoon ground turmeric

½ teaspoon fenugreek powder, blue if you can get it

scant ½ cup good-quality sunflower oil

1 lemon

2 oz feta cheese

4 sprigs of tarragon

1 pomegranate

1 scant cup Greek yogurt

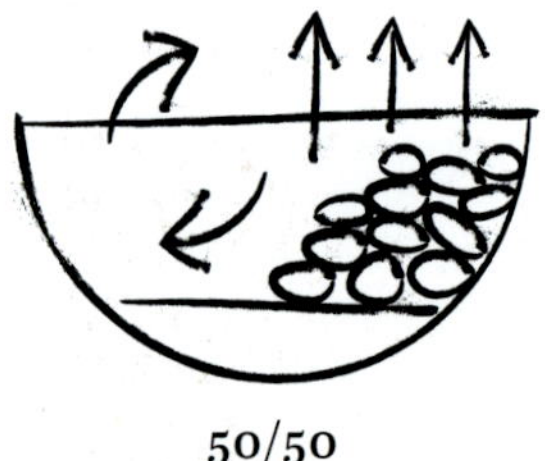

50/50

I was introduced to nigvziani badrijani, a popular stuffed eggplant dish, by Georgian chef Guram Baghdoshvili. It's traditionally eaten cold or at room temperature, but eggplant is so good grilled that I had to include this.

1 Slice the eggplants lengthwise ¼ inch thick, then, in a single layer, sprinkle generously with sea salt, and cover with paper towels and something heavy.

2 To make the stuffing, bash the walnuts in a mortar and pestle with the peeled garlic, turmeric and fenugreek until fine, then muddle in the sunflower oil to make a paste. Set up a fine sieve over a bowl, spoon in the paste, and push it through the sieve, capturing the golden oil in the bowl below. Set the oil aside and scrape the paste back into the mortar. Muddle in half the lemon juice and most of the feta. Pick and finely chop half the tarragon leaves, then stir in. Halve the pomegranate and, holding one half cut side down in the palm of your hand, bash the back with a spoon so all the seeds tumble out into the mortar, reserving the other half. Light the grill (pages 16–19).

3 Pat the eggplant slices dry, brush with a little olive oil, then grill on the hot zone for 5 minutes, or until softened and lightly charred, flipping halfway – you may need to work in batches. Transfer to a board and spread the slices evenly with the stuffing, then roll up and double skewer across 2 long metal skewers. Rub with 1 tablespoon of olive oil, season with salt and spritz with red wine vinegar. Cook for 8 minutes on the hot zone, turning regularly and moving to the cooler zone if they're coloring too quickly.

4 Hold the remaining pomegranate half cut side down in the palm of your hand and bash the back with a spoon so all the seeds tumble out into a bowl. Mix the yogurt with the remaining lemon juice, season, and spread it onto a serving board. Place the eggplants on top, then cut between the skewers and remove them. Drizzle on 1 tablespoon of the golden oil (save the rest for salads, grilled meats and fish), pick and sprinkle with the remaining tarragon, scatter on the pomegranate seeds and crumble on the remaining feta.

Brunch bits

Glazed rum pineapple

Serves 4 | 30 minutes

⅓ cup unsalted roasted peanuts

1 ripe pineapple

2 limes

4 tablespoons unsalted butter

scant ¼ cup spiced rum

3 tablespoons runny honey

optional: 1 bunch of thyme (about ⅔ oz)

¼ cup Greek or coconut yogurt

1 Light the grill (pages 16–19). Crush the peanuts in a mortar and pestle, toast them in a small cast-iron frying pan on the hot zone until golden, then transfer to a bowl, removing the pan from the heat.

2 Top and tail the pineapple, then slice the peel off the sides and halve lengthwise. Finely grate the lime zest and put most of it into the pan, reserving a little for garnish, then squeeze in the juice and add the butter.

3 Grill the pineapple halves on the hot zone for 20 to 25 minutes, turning regularly with tongs until golden and caramelized, moving them to the medium and cool zones as needed to control how quickly they color.

4 Place the pan on the medium zone until the butter has melted, is starting to smell nutty and looks foamy. Add the rum, flame it if you like (stand back!), then stir in the honey and use the mixture to glaze the pineapple as it cooks – I like to use a bunch of thyme as a brush for bonus fragrance. Toss the toasted nuts into the residual glaze in the pan for the last minute.

5 Spread the yogurt onto a serving platter, transfer the pineapple to a board and chop it up, removing and discarding the core, then pile onto the platter, spoon on the sticky nuts and sprinkle with the reserved lime zest.

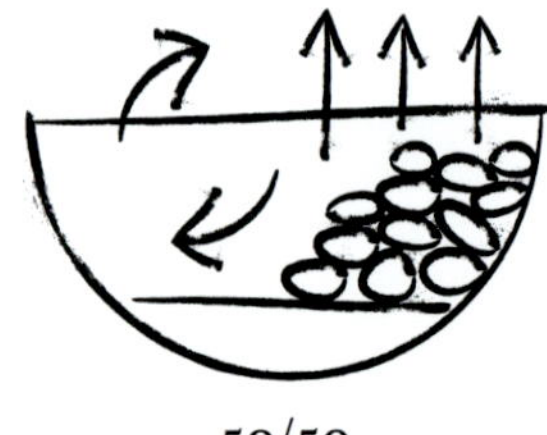

50/50

Ultimate barbecue brekkie

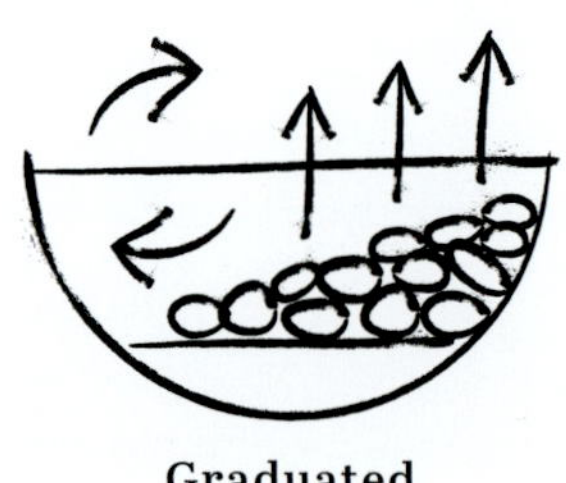

Graduated

You can either go all out and cook up every recipe on these pages, creating an ultimate breakfast feast – and I've tried it, so trust me, it really does all fit on a regular grill. Or, you can pick and choose whichever elements excite you to make up your own perfect brekkie – I also like to include a few corn (page 124) or halloumi fritters (page 130), like you see in the picture. Everything can be easily scaled up or down depending on how many hungry mouths you're feeding. And obviously, if you're cooking for veggie friends, it's polite to get the veggie stuff on the grill first, then follow up with the meat when it's done. Have fun!

Crispy bacon & sizzling sausages

Serves 4 | **25 minutes**

Light the grill (pages 16–19). Line up **4 pork sausages**. Peel and quarter **1 small red onion**, break apart into petals, and poke the petals in between the sausages along with the leaves from **2 sprigs of sage**. Carefully poke 2 long metal skewers through all the sausages, meaning you can cook and turn them as one. Take **8 slices of thick-cut bacon** and thread the end of each slice onto another long metal skewer so it dangles like a flag. Cook it all on the hot zone for 2 minutes, or until nicely colored, moving the sausage skewers to the cool zone to cook through for 20 minutes, turning halfway, and laying the bacon on top to prevent it getting too crispy.

Go veggie: Simply ditch the bacon, and swap in your favorite veggie sausages, spritzing regularly with olive oil as they cook.

Dotty coddled egg peppers

Serves 4 | **30 minutes**

Light the grill (pages 16–19). Halve and seed **2 bell peppers**, leaving the stems attached for easier handling. Grill cut side down on the hot zone with the lid on, vents open, for 15 minutes, or until starting to soften, adding **4 oz of ripe cherry tomatoes on the vine** to cook alongside for the last 5 minutes. Flip the peppers, then season with a little sea salt and black pepper. Take **4 eggs** and crack one into each pepper half, divide the tomatoes among them, then spritz with olive oil. Cook on the hot zone with the lid on, vents open, for 10 to 15 minutes, or until the peppers are soft and the eggs are cooked to your liking, carefully moving to the medium zone if they're coloring too quickly.

Tomato bread

Serves 4 | 20 minutes

Light the grill (pages 16–19). Place **8 oz of ripe cherry tomatoes on the vine** on the medium zone to cook with the lid on, vents open, for 5 minutes, or until softened and charred. Grill **2 thick slices of sourdough bread** on the cool zone until lightly toasted on each side, then remove. Halve **1 clove of garlic** and rub each hot toast once with the cut side, then drizzle with extra virgin olive oil. Use tongs or a fork to smush and rub the soft tomatoes onto both sides of the bread, discarding the vines. Return to the grill (or cast-iron pan, if using for other things) on the hot zone until wonderfully charred on each side, moving to the cooler zone if coloring too quickly. Slice, and serve.

Bubbling baked beans

Serves 4 | 15 minutes

Light the grill (pages 16–19). Simply open **2 x 15-oz cans of baked beans** and place them on the cool zone. Let them bubble away while the rest of your brekkie cooks, carefully stirring occasionally, until heated through. Carefully remove the hot cans from the grill and season to perfection with dashes of **Worcestershire and Tabasco sauce**.

Stuffed mushrooms

Serves 4 | 25 minutes

Light the grill (pages 16–19) and preheat a cast-iron pan on the cool zone. Trim **4 portobello mushrooms**, then grill on the hot zone, stem side down, with the lid on, vents open, for 10 minutes, or until softened. Very thinly slice, then roughly chop **4 oz of halloumi cheese**. Finely grate on the zest of **½ a lemon**, tear on the leaves from **2 sprigs of basil**, drizzle with 1 teaspoon of olive oil, season with black pepper and scrunch together. Flip the mushrooms, season, transfer them to the hot skillet, then divide the halloumi mixture among them. Carefully move the pan to the hot zone and cook with the lid on, vents open, for 10 to 15 minutes, or until melty and delicious, carefully moving the skillet to the medium zone if they're coloring too quickly.

Corn fritters

Serves 4 | 25 minutes

⅔ cup fresh or canned, drained corn kernels

½ cup cottage cheese

⅔ cup coarse cornmeal

¾ cup self-rising flour (see note on page 84)

3 tablespoons reduced-fat milk

½ teaspoon baking powder

2 large eggs

¼ cup jarred sliced jalapeños

1 ripe avocado

1 lime

3 ripe mixed-color tomatoes

2 sprigs of basil

¼ cup Greek yogurt

chili oil or chili jam, to serve

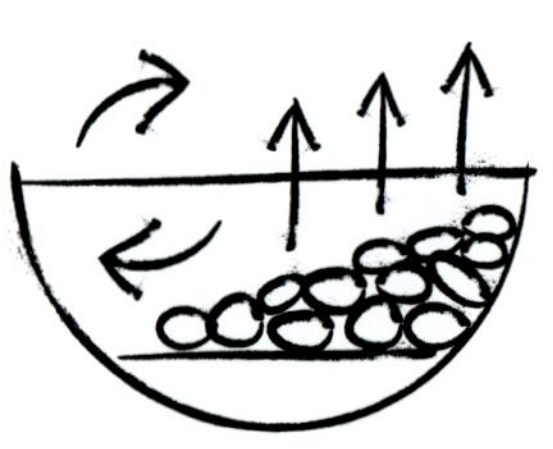

Graduated

1 Add the corn to a large bowl along with the cottage cheese, cornmeal, flour, milk and baking powder. Crack in the eggs and add the jalapeños, along with 3 tablespoons of juice from the jar. Add 3 tablespoons of olive oil, season with sea salt and black pepper, and mix well. Light the grill (pages 16–19). Preheat a cast-iron pan on the cool zone.

2 Carefully move the pan to the hot zone, spritz with oil and, in batches or to order, cook tablespoons of the batter – about 4 to 5 per person – for 2 to 3 minutes on each side, or until golden and cooked through, carefully moving the skillet to the medium zone if the fritters are coloring too quickly.

3 Meanwhile, halve, pit, peel and slice the avo, then dress with lime juice and season to perfection. Thinly slice the tomatoes. Divide it all among your plates, tear on the basil leaves and dollop on the yogurt. Pile the fritters on top and drizzle with chili oil. This is wonderful in its own right, but also makes a lovely addition to my Ultimate barbecue brekkie (pages 118–123).

BBQ baked beans

Serves 8–10 | 45 minutes

½ x Pantry BBQ sauce (page 202)

2 cloves of garlic

1 x 16-oz jar of roasted red peppers

1 bunch of sage (about ⅔ oz)

1 lb fresh or frozen chopped mixed onion, carrot & celery

1 x 14.5-oz can of cherry tomatoes

2 x 15-oz cans of kidney, navy, cannellini or borlotti beans, or a combination

1 Make the Pantry BBQ sauce (page 202). Peel and thinly slice the garlic. Drain and finely chop the peppers. Light the grill (pages 16–19).

2 Put a large deep cast-iron pan on the hot zone, add 2 tablespoons of olive oil, and pick in the sage leaves. Fry until crispy, then use tongs or a slotted spoon to transfer half the sage leaves to paper towels for later.

3 Add the garlic, stirring regularly, and, once lightly golden, add the chopped mixed veg. Cook for 5 to 10 minutes, or until starting to color, then pour in the tomatoes, breaking them up with your spoon. Add the chopped peppers, the beans, juices and all, and the BBQ sauce. Once it starts bubbling, carefully move to the medium zone and simmer with the grill lid on, vents open, for 30 minutes, or until thickened, stirring occasionally.

4 Season the beans to perfection with sea salt and black pepper, and serve sprinkled with the reserved crispy sage. Great with fresh bread, grilled toasts, or piled onto tortillas or tacos. Lovely with a fried egg, or you could even crack some eggs into the beans to cook for the last few minutes. Also a dream dished up with my Ultimate barbecue brekkie (pages 118–123).

Helpful hint: If you don't have the grill lit for other things, you can absolutely cook this inside on the stove, if you prefer.

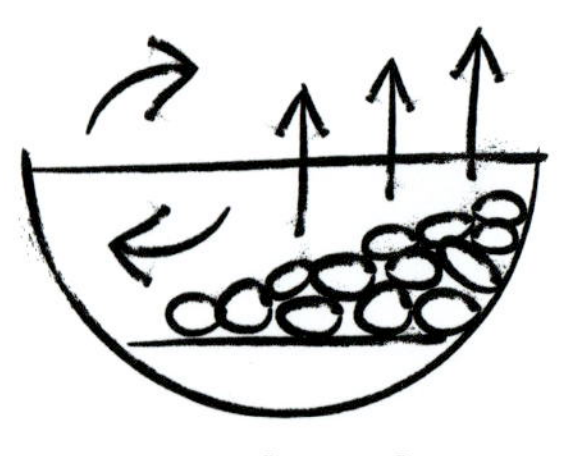

Graduated

Grilled black pepper peaches

Serves 4 | **20 minutes**

1 cup ricotta cheese

2 tablespoons runny honey

1 lemon

4 ripe peaches

4 slices of panettone or brioche (about 12 oz)

1 Add the ricotta and honey to a bowl and beat until smooth. Finely grate in the lemon zest and beat again until you have a whipped consistency. Halve and pit the peaches. Light the grill (pages 16–19).

2 Spritz the peach halves with olive oil, then grill on the hot zone until beautifully charred, turning with tongs. Move them to the medium-cool zone and cook for 10 minutes with the lid on, vents open, or until softened.

3 Briefly toast the panettone slices on the hot zone, then transfer to serving plates and top with the grilled peaches. Spoon on the whipped ricotta and season with a generous pinch of black pepper (trust me!). Finish with a little squeeze of lemon and a few drops of extra virgin olive oil, if you like.

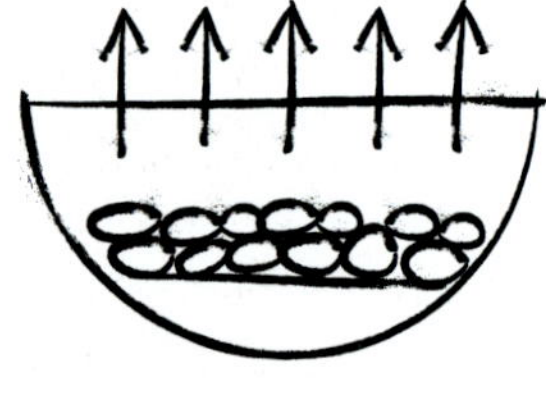

Flat

Halloumi fritters

Serves 6 | 40 minutes

2 large eggs

1¾ cups self-rising flour (see note on page 84)

⅔ cup reduced-fat milk

12 mixed-color olives, with pits

1 English cucumber

1 large slice of watermelon

1 lemon

1 fresh red chili

4 scallions

8 oz halloumi cheese

1 bunch of mint (about 1 oz)

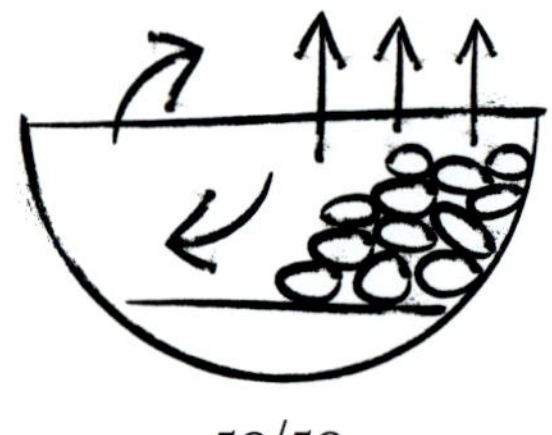

1 Light the grill (pages 16–19). In a large bowl, whisk the eggs into the flour with a pinch of sea salt, then gradually whisk in the milk until smooth.

2 For the salsa, smash and pit the olives, then finely chop. Roughly peel the cucumber with a vegetable peeler, halve it lengthwise and use a teaspoon to scrape out the seedy core, then chop into ½-inch chunks. Peel and dice the watermelon into ½-inch chunks. Scrape it all into a bowl, ready to dress later.

3 Thinly slice the lemon, prick the chili, trim the scallions, then place it all on the hot zone with the block of halloumi. Use tongs to turn it all until lightly charred, transferring it to your board as it's done. Finely chop the lemon, chop up the scallions, scrape the skin off the chili, seed and thinly slice it, and chop up the halloumi. Scrape it all into the bowl of batter, pick, roughly chop and add most of the mint leaves, and mix together.

4 Put a large shallow cast-iron pan on the medium-hot zone. Spritz with olive oil and add spoonfuls of batter, spreading them out to a scant 1 inch thick. Cook for 3 minutes on each side, or until dark golden and cooked through, moving the fritters to the cool zone of the grill to keep warm while you cook the rest.

5 Pick the remaining mint leaves into the salsa, toss it all with 1 tablespoon each of red wine vinegar and extra virgin olive oil, and season to perfection. Quarter the fritters and serve with the salsa. Great with a fried egg, or on a bed of plain yogurt swirled with Chili sauce (page 204).

Epic feasts

Barbecued meat chilli

Serves 12 | 3 hours

1 teaspoon cumin seeds

4 cloves of garlic

1 x 3.5-oz jar of chipotle chili paste

6 bone-in, skin-on chicken thighs (1¾ lbs)

1¾-lb piece of boneless pork shoulder, fat trimmed

1¾ lbs skirt steak

3 mixed-color bell peppers

6 jalapeños

4 stalks of celery

1 bunch of scallions

3 x 14.5-oz cans of whole tomatoes

3½ cups hot coffee

1½ x 13-oz jars of butter or cannellini beans

½ a bunch of cilantro (about ½ oz)

1 Light the grill (pages 16–19) and soak a handful of wood chips according to the package instructions. In a mortar and pestle, pound the cumin seeds with 2 teaspoons each of sea salt and black pepper until fine. Peel and pound in the garlic, then muddle in the chili paste. Put the chicken, pork and steak into a large deep cast-iron pan, add the chili paste mixture, and massage well.

2 Prick the peppers and jalapeños, then lightly char on the medium zone with the celery and scallions, transferring to your board once nicely marked.

3 Place all the meat directly on the hot or medium zone for 10 minutes, or until seared all over, turning regularly with tongs, while you trim and slice the scallions and celery, halve and seed the jalapeños, and roughly chop the peppers, discarding the seeds and stems.

4 Scrape the veg into the empty pan and place on the medium zone. Add the seared meat, then pour in the tomatoes and coffee. Cover the pan, then put the grill lid on, top vent half open, and cook for 2 hours – the temperature of the barbecue should sit at around 350°F.

5 Carefully remove the pan lid, then stir in the beans, juices and all. Drain the wood chips and place on the hot zone. Cook with the grill lid on, vents open, for 30 minutes, then stir well and check that the meat is tender and pullable.

6 Shred all the meat, discarding the chicken bones and skin. Finely chop and stir in the cilantro leaves with 1 tablespoon of red wine vinegar, then season to perfection. Great served with rice, yogurt, Chili sauce (page 204) and chunks of lime-dressed avo, if you fancy.

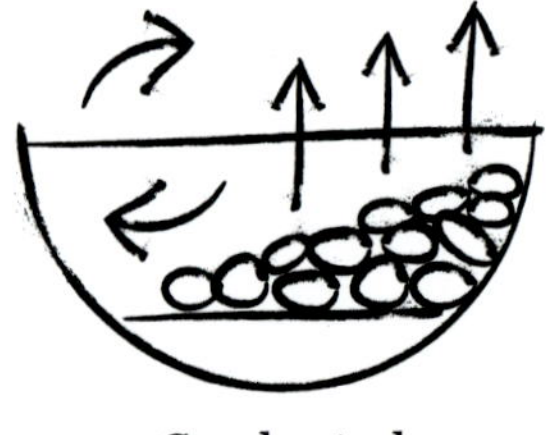

Graduated

Helpful hint: Fill the empty chipotle chili paste jar with olive oil, give it a good shake and you can use it to add bonus flavor to all sorts of dishes!

Juicy pork belly, fennel & orange salad

Serves 10 | Prep 10 minutes | Cook 5 hours, plus resting

4½-lb piece of pork belly, skin on, bone in (or 4 lb boneless)

1 big bunch of mixed woody herbs (about 2 oz), such as oregano, marjoram, sage, thyme, rosemary

2 lemons

2 firm pears

1 bulb of fennel

2 stalks of celery

2 oranges

⅔ cup black olives, with pits

1 fresh red chili

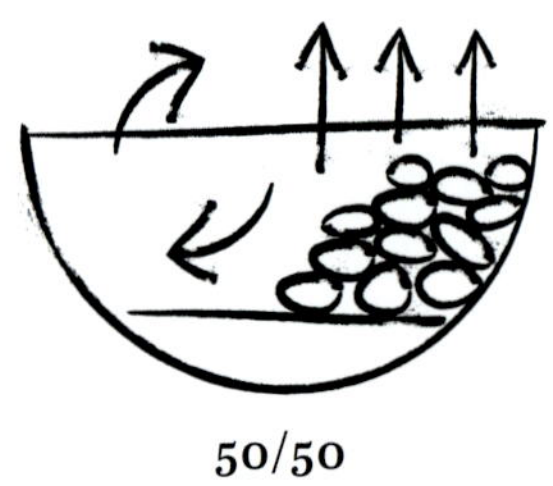

50/50

1 Light the grill (pages 16–19). Place a roasting pan with 2 cups of water underneath the grate in the cool zone – this will help the pork steam and you'll also capture the beautiful juices in the pan as it cooks.

2 Use a skewer or sharp knife to stab all over the skin of the pork belly (don't score it, as that will release too much fat). Rub all over with 2 teaspoons of sea salt, getting it into the openings, then place on the hot zone for 5 minutes, or until golden brown all over, turning regularly with tongs. Transfer to a board.

3 Strip half the herb leaves into a mortar and pestle and pound to a paste. Muddle in the juice of ½ a lemon, reserving the squeezed half, and 4 tablespoons of olive oil, then pour over and massage into the pork.

4 Place the pork skin side down on the cool zone. Rub the remaining herb sprigs in the leftover herb oil on the board and tuck them, along with the squeezed lemon half, under the side of the pork closest to the coals to protect it as it cooks. Cook for 5 hours with the lid on, top vent half open, or until gnarly and meltingly tender, checking occasionally and topping up the pan with more water if it looks dry. The grill temperature should start at around 475°F, then you want it to settle between 350°F and 400°F for another 1½ to 2 hours, then it will continue to drop to about 300°F; adjust your coals or gas as needed. Once cooked, remove the pork, then carefully remove the grate and the pan of juices. Place the pork in the pan to rest for 30 minutes.

5 To make a fresh, delicate salad, very thinly slice the pears, fennel (reserving any fronds) and celery with a vegetable peeler or good knife skills. Peel the oranges and slice into thin rounds. Squeeze on the juice of 1 lemon, add 1 tablespoon of extra virgin olive oil, gently toss together, then season to perfection and spread onto a serving platter. Smash, pit and finely chop the olives with the chili (seed, if you like), then dress with ½ tablespoon of extra virgin olive oil and the remaining lemon juice.

6 Slice the pork and lay on the salad, spooning on any resting juices. Sprinkle with the chopped olives and any reserved fennel fronds. It's worth the wait!

Gnarly sirloin roast with salsa, rice & beans

Serves 10 | **Prep 15 minutes** | **Cook 50 minutes, plus resting**

2 red onions

3 oz cured chorizo

2½ cups basmati rice

6 fresh bay leaves

1 x 15-oz can of cannellini beans

1 x 3- to 3½-lb boneless top sirloin roast

½ a bunch of rosemary (about ⅓ oz)

½ a ripe pineapple (about 14 oz) or 1 x 14-oz can of pineapple in juice

2 red bell peppers

1 lb ripe tomatoes

½ a bunch of mint (about ½ oz)

4 cups baby arugula

1 Light the grill (pages 16–19). Peel and finely chop ½ an onion, reserving the rest, finely chop the chorizo, then add it all to a Dutch oven with the rice and bay leaves. Pour in the beans, juices and all, along with 1½ cans of water and a pinch of sea salt. Stir well.

2 Score the fat on top of the beef in a crosshatch pattern to help it render quickly. Season generously with salt and black pepper, then place on the medium zone with the rosemary sprigs underneath. Brown for 10 minutes in total, turning occasionally with tongs, until colored on all sides – if it flares up, carefully move to the cooler zone.

3 Carefully remove the grate and place the rice pan directly in the cool zone. Replace the grate, then place the meat fat side down on the grate, over the pan. Cook with the lid on, top vent half open above the meat for 40 to 50 minutes for blushing medium-rare – the internal temperature should be 130°F.

4 Meanwhile, peel and finely dice the remaining onions and the pineapple and scrape onto a serving platter big enough for the beef. Seed and finely dice the peppers, finely dice the tomatoes and add it all to the platter, then pick, finely chop and add the mint leaves. Dress with 1 tablespoon each of red wine vinegar and extra virgin olive oil and season to perfection.

5 Rest the meat on top of the salsa for at least 30 minutes – the internal temperature should reach 140°F. Carefully remove the rice pan, and cover until serving. Slice the meat a scant ½ inch thick, drizzle with a little extra virgin olive oil and season with salt. Serve with the salsa, rice and beans, and the arugula.

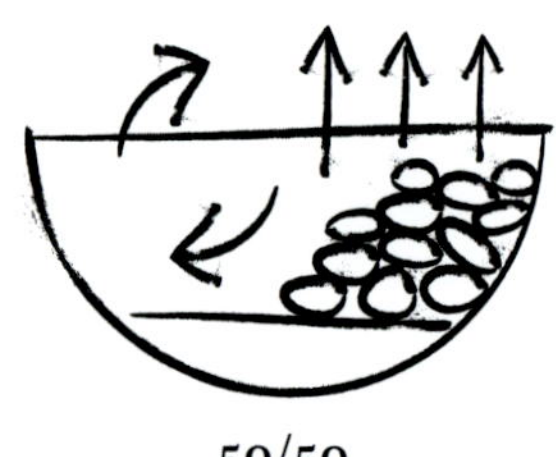

50/50

Arrabiatta chicken drumsticks

Serves 6 | 1 hour 15 minutes

4 cloves of garlic

2 large onions

6 fresh red chilies

12 chicken drumsticks

4 fresh bay leaves

3 oz thick-cut bacon, cut into scant ½-inch pieces

1 lemon

2 lbs ripe tomatoes

2 tablespoons tomato paste

½ cup vodka

1 Light the grill (pages 16–19). Peel and slice the garlic cloves. Peel and halve the onions. Prick the chilies. Drizzle the chicken with 1 tablespoon of olive oil and season with sea salt and black pepper.

2 Put a large shallow cast-iron pan on the medium zone and add 1 tablespoon of oil, the garlic, bay and bacon. Use a vegetable peeler to add the lemon peel in strips, and fry it all until lightly golden, stirring regularly.

3 Alongside, grill the halved onions, whole chilies and tomatoes for 8 to 10 minutes, or until softened and nicely marked, then transfer to a board. Adding to the pan as you go, chop the onions into rough ½-inch chunks, squash or chop up the tomatoes, and seed, slice and add the chilies, scraping off the larger bits of blackened skin. Stir in the tomato paste.

4 Grill the chicken on the hot zone for 10 minutes, or until golden all over, turning regularly with tongs, then nestle into the pan. Add the vodka and flame it, if you like (stand back!). Squeeze in the lemon juice, then cook with the lid on, vents open, for 45 minutes, or until the chicken is cooked through. Great with a side salad, and rice, couscous or crusty bread to mop up all those delicious juices.

Epic chicken arrabiatta sandwich

Make **My favorite focaccia** (page 226), halve it horizontally, and you can use this dish to make the most epic of epic sarnies! Simply shred all the meat, discarding the bones, then spread the arrabiatta sauce over the bottom of the focaccia, piling the meat on top. Sprinkle on a layer of **arugula**, tear on **1 x 4-oz ball of mozzarella cheese**, use a vegetable peeler to add a few shavings of **Parmesan cheese**, then sandwich together, slice and serve. I like to finely grate on a bit of extra Parmesan for a fancy finish, too. Great for 12 very lucky people. Check the pictures on the following pages for inspo!

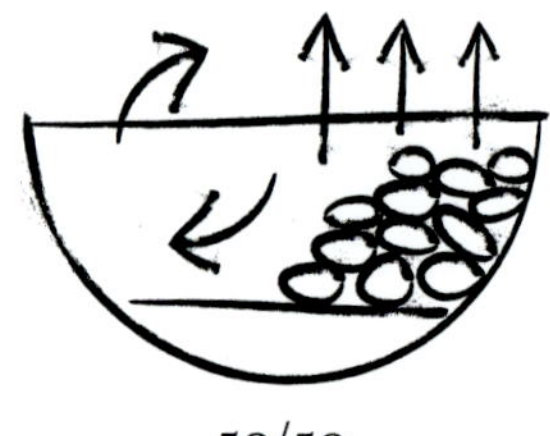

50/50

Classic leg of lamb

Serves 10 | Prep 10 minutes | Cook 1 hour 15 minutes, plus resting

6½-lb leg of lamb, bone in, frenched (ask your butcher)

6 cloves of garlic

2 large lemons

1 bunch of sage (about ⅔ oz)

1 x 2-oz tin of anchovy fillets in oil

6 large red onions

2 lbs ripe mixed-color tomatoes

1 Use a small sharp knife to make 6 deep incisions into each side of the lamb (12 in total), poking your finger into each to make little pockets.

2 Peel and halve the garlic cloves. Use a vegetable peeler to strip off 12 pieces of lemon peel. Pick and lay out 12 large sage leaves, then divide the garlic, anchovies and lemon peel among them. Drizzle with the oil from the anchovy tin, then roll up each stack and stuff into the pockets in the lamb. Season all over with sea salt and black pepper. Light the grill (pages 16–19).

3 Halve the unpeeled onions through the root. Place the lamb in the center of the grill with the onion halves snugly around it, cut side up. Cook with the lid on, top vent half open, for 1 hour 15 minutes, or until the internal temperature reaches 130°F, checking after 1 hour. Transfer to a plate with the onions and let rest, covered, for 30 minutes (the internal temp should rise to 140°F).

4 Thinly slice the tomatoes and arrange on a large serving board. Pinch off and discard the skins of the soft onions, add the onions to the board, then place the lamb on top. Pour on any resting juices, squeeze on the lemon juice, carve, and serve. Cute with a few chive flowers on top, if you've got them. Delicious with a multitude of things, including my Grilled caponata (page 90), Med-style greens (page 92) or Salsa verde (page 206). Enjoy!

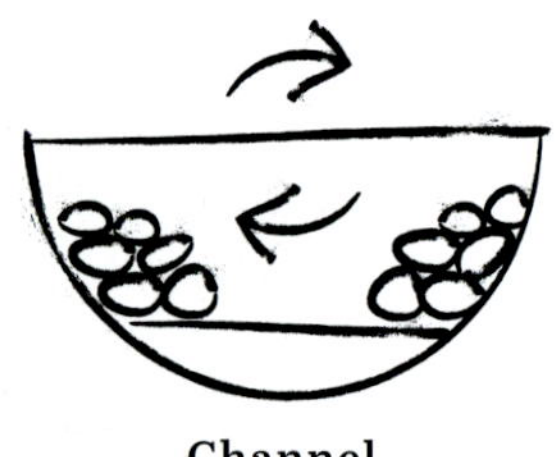

Channel

Herby grilled veg, halloumi skewers & pancakes

Serves 8 | 45 minutes, plus resting

2 cups bread flour

2¼ teaspoons instant or rapid-rise yeast

2 tablespoons runny honey

1 eggplant (about 14 oz)

2 zucchini

1 red onion (6 oz)

2 red bell peppers (12 oz total)

1 bulb of fennel

1½ cups ripe mixed-color cherry tomatoes

1¼ cups mixed unsalted nuts

1 clove of garlic

½ cup dried cranberries

1 bunch of mixed soft herbs (about 1 oz)

8 oz halloumi cheese

2 mixed-color chilies

1 lemon

½ cup Greek yogurt

½ a pomegranate

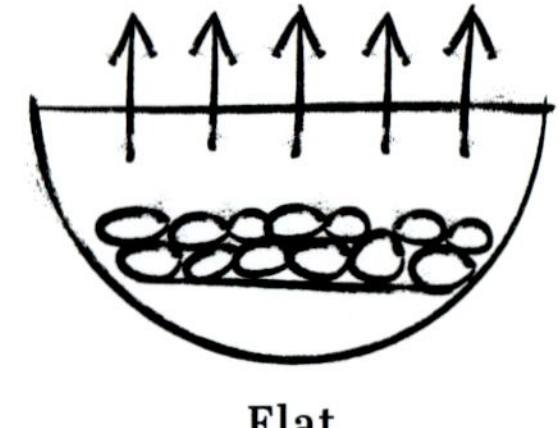

Flat

1 Light the grill (pages 16–19). Add the flour to a bowl with 1 teaspoon of sea salt and the yeast, then whisk in 2 cups of lukewarm water, the honey and 2 tablespoons of olive oil. Cover and let sit for 30 minutes to do its thing (near the warmth of the grill is great!) – it should be aerated and bubbly.

2 Slice the eggplant and zucchini a scant ¼ inch thick lengthwise. Peel the onion and slice into ¼-inch rounds. Cut the bell peppers into similar-sized pieces, discarding the seeds and stems. Halve the fennel lengthwise, then cut into scant ½-inch-thick wedges, reserving any fronds. Working in batches, grill all the veg and tomatoes for 4 minutes, or until softened and charred, turning halfway, and transferring to a board once done.

3 For the dressing, blitz the nuts, peeled garlic clove, dried cranberries, most of the herb leaves, 1½ tablespoons of red wine vinegar and 3 tablespoons of extra virgin olive oil to a coarse paste in a food processor, then season to perfection. Roughly chop the eggplant and zucchini, then toss all the veg with the dressing on a nice big serving platter.

4 Dice most of the halloumi into ¾-inch chunks, reserving a little, and slice the chilies ¾ inch thick, then skewer it all up – I like to use little rosemary skewers for bonus flavor. Preheat a large shallow cast-iron pan on the grill. Spritz with olive oil and pour in 2 ladles of batter – it will spread out like a thin pancake. After 1 minute, spritz it with oil and finely grate on a little lemon zest and reserved halloumi. Cook for 4 minutes, then flip for just 2 minutes on the other side. Remove and repeat with the remaining batter. Grill the halloumi skewers on the grate alongside, turning until golden.

5 To serve, dollop the yogurt over the dressed veg, then, holding the pomegranate half cut side down in the palm of your hand, bash the back with a spoon so all the seeds tumble out over the top. Pick and sprinkle on the remaining herbs and any reserved fennel fronds, add the halloumi skewers and serve with the pancakes for tearing and scooping!

Grilled chili & lemon chicken

Serves 6 | Prep 30 minutes | Cook 1 hour, plus resting

9 mixed-color chilies

1 long sweet red pepper

1 bulb of garlic

4 fresh bay leaves

½ teaspoon dried red chili flakes

1 bunch of thyme (about ⅔ oz)

1 lemon

1 x 3½-lb whole chicken

optional: sprigs of bay, thyme, rosemary

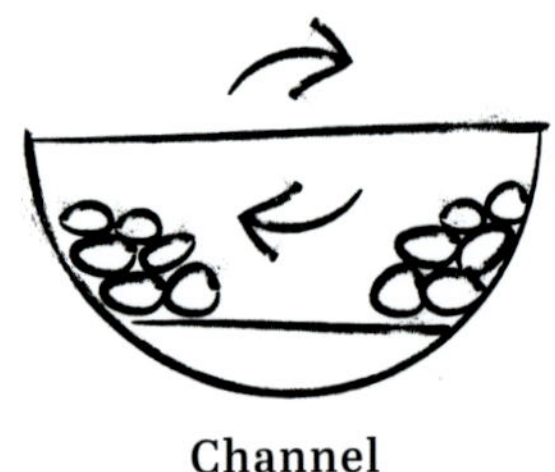

Channel

Bringing piri piri vibes, here we're making an incredible sauce to use as both a marinade for cooking and a salsa to serve, meaning double flavor impact.

1 Light the grill (pages 16–19). Prick the chilies and red pepper and, as the barbecue heats up, char the chilies, red pepper and whole garlic bulb over the hot zone with the lid on, vents open.

2 Use tongs to toast the bay leaves on the grill for 30 seconds, then tear into a mortar and pestle, discarding the stems. Add the chili flakes and a pinch of sea salt, strip in the thyme and pound well. Use a vegetable peeler to strip in the lemon peel and pound again into a rough paste (you can use a small food processor for this step, if you prefer). Remove the thick white pith from the lemon, then finely chop the flesh. Muddle into the mortar and pestle with 2 tablespoons each of red wine vinegar and extra virgin olive oil.

3 Scrape off the larger bits of charred skin from the chilies and red pepper, discarding the seeds and stems, peel the garlic, then finely chop it all. Scrape into the mortar and pestle, mix together and season to perfection.

4 Use a large sharp knife to carefully cut down one side of the chicken's backbone, so you can open it out flat like a book, then score the legs. Reserve half the sauce in a small bowl for serving, then rub the rest over the chicken, getting into all the nooks and crannies. Place on the cool zone, skin side up, tucking extra woody herb sprigs around the edges to protect the chicken as it cooks, if you like, and cook with the lid on, vents open, for 1 hour, or until juicy and cooked through and the internal temperature of the breast is at least 160°F. Transfer to a clean board to rest for 30 minutes (the internal temp needs to reach 165°F in the breast and 175°F in the thigh).

5 Spoon on the remaining sauce and carve up the chicken. Great with Grilled fries (page 222) or sweet potato wedges, or my Sriracha corn (page 94).

Herby leg of lamb & creamy beans

Serves 10 | Prep 25 minutes | Cook 1 hour, plus resting

4 leeks

1 bunch of mixed soft herbs (about 1 oz), such as mint, tarragon, basil, parsley

2 cloves of garlic

½ cup shelled unsalted pistachios

2 lemons

¾ cup fine dried breadcrumbs

4½- to 5-lb butterflied leg of lamb, boned (ask your butcher to do this for you)

2 tablespoons Dijon mustard

1 bunch of sage (about ⅔ oz)

1½ cups ripe cherry tomatoes

3 x 15-oz cans of cannellini beans

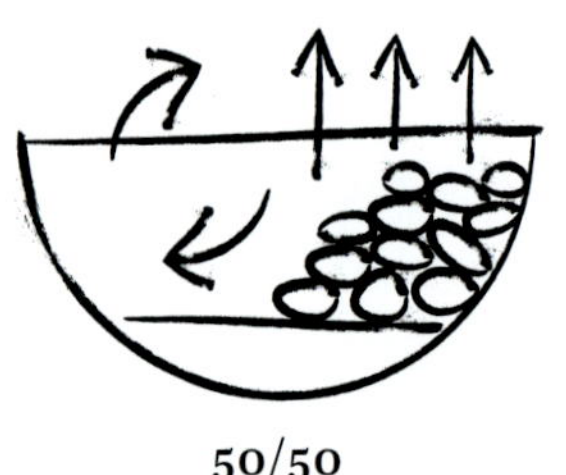

50/50

1 Soak a handful of wood chips in water according to the package instructions. Light the grill (pages 16–19). Blacken the leeks directly on the coals for 10 to 15 minutes, turning halfway, then transfer to a board.

2 Meanwhile, pick the soft herb leaves into a mortar and pestle with a pinch of sea salt, pound into a coarse paste, then peel and pound in the garlic. Roughly pound in the pistachios, then muddle in 2 tablespoons of extra virgin olive oil, squeeze in the juice of 1 lemon and scrunch in the breadcrumbs until combined (blitz in a food processor, if you prefer).

3 Lay the lamb out like an open book and massage all over with salt, black pepper and 1 tablespoon of olive oil. Sear on the hot zone for 5 minutes, or until gnarly, turning regularly with tongs, then transfer to a board, skin side down. Massage the top with the mustard, then pat on the herby crumbs.

4 Peel off and discard the outer charred layers of the leeks, cut into ¾-inch lengths and add to an 8- x 10-inch baking pan (or equivalent). Rub half the sage leaves with olive oil, then add to the pan with the tomatoes and a generous splash of water. Carefully remove the grate and place the pan directly in the cool zone. Replace the grate, then place the lamb, crumb side up, on the grate over the pan. Halve the remaining lemon and tuck it under the side of the lamb nearest the coals. Drain the wood chips and place on the hot zone with the remaining sage sprigs. Cook with the lid on, top vent half open above the meat for 30 minutes.

5 Carefully lift up the lamb and the grate and pour the beans into the pan, juices and all. Replace the grate and lamb and cook for another 10 to 15 minutes with the lid on, top vent half open, or until the internal temperature of the lamb reaches 130°F. Remove the lamb and let rest, covered, for 30 minutes (the internal temp should rise to 140°F), leaving the beans to reduce for another 15 minutes.

6 Mix 1 tablespoon of red wine vinegar into the beans, season to perfection, then slice and add the lamb. Great with crusty bread and a green salad.

Pulled beef tacos

Serves 10 | Prep 30 minutes | Cook 3 hours

4 cloves

2 fresh bay leaves

2 teaspoons English or Dijon mustard

2½ to 3 lbs beef shanks, bone in

3 red onions

2 large carrots

10 slices of bacon

1 bunch of mixed woody herbs (about ⅔ oz), such as sage, rosemary

1 heaping teaspoon orange marmalade

⅔ cup Worcestershire sauce

optional: 4 pickled walnuts

2 apples

¼ a medium head of green cabbage (8 oz)

3 oz watercress (about 3 cups)

4 limes

10 mini flour tortillas

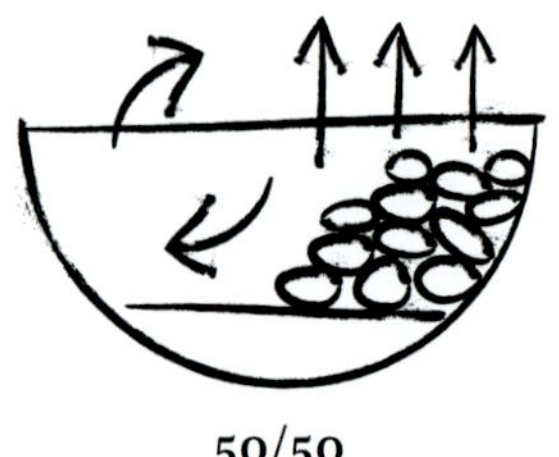

50/50

1 Light the grill (pages 16–19). Put 1 teaspoon of sea salt and 2 teaspoons of black pepper into a mortar and pestle with the cloves and bay (stems removed) and pound well, then muddle in the mustard and 2 tablespoons of olive oil to make a paste. Rub it all over the beef, then place on the hot zone for 25 minutes, turning with tongs to build up a nice crust, and moving it from the hot to the medium zone as needed to control how quickly it colors.

2 Peel, halve and add 2 onions to the grill, turning with tongs until nicely marked, then transfer to a board and chop into rough ½-inch chunks. Chop the carrots a similar size. Slice the bacon and add to a large deep cast-iron pan on the hot zone with 1 tablespoon of olive oil. Strip in the herb leaves and cook until golden, stirring occasionally.

3 Add the chopped onions and carrots and cook for 10 minutes, stirring regularly, then stir in the marmalade and Worcestershire sauce. Thinly slice and add the walnuts, if using, then use tongs to transfer the beef to the pan and carefully move to the cool zone. Put the lid on the pan, and the grill lid on, top vent half open. Cook for 2 hours 30 minutes, or until the meat easily pulls apart. Halfway through, add a splash of water to the pan and baste the meat. The grill temperature should sit at around 350°F throughout.

4 Matchstick the apples, use a sharp knife or a vegetable peeler to thinly shred the cabbage, peel and finely chop the remaining onion. Pile on a plate with the watercress, squeeze on the juice of 2 limes and add a pinch of salt.

5 Use tongs to – one by one – wipe one side of the tortillas through the fat on the surface of the pan, then place on the cool zone of the grill. Use two forks to pull the meat apart, then shake the marrow out of the bone and mix in. Season to perfection, then serve it all at the table with the jar of mustard and the remaining lime wedges, and let everyone build their own.

Pomegranate & harissa chicken

Serves 6 | Prep 10 minutes, plus marinating | Cook 1 hour 10 minutes, plus resting

1 onion

2 cloves of garlic

1 pomegranate

2 tablespoons rose harissa

3 tablespoons runny honey

1 x 3½-lb whole chicken

1 lemon

optional: 1 bunch of woody herbs (about ⅔ oz) such as rosemary, thyme

1 Peel and roughly chop the onion and garlic and add it all to a blender. Halve the pomegranate and, holding one half cut side down in the palm of your hand, bash the back with a spoon so all the seeds tumble out into the blender, reserving the other half. Add the harissa, honey, 2 tablespoons of olive oil and a pinch each of sea salt and black pepper, and blitz until smooth.

2 Reserving a quarter of the sauce, rub the rest over the chicken really well. Let marinate for 30 minutes. Light the grill (pages 16–19).

3 Place the chicken, breast side down, on the cool zone, so the breasts are in the middle and the legs are closer to the hot zone on either side. Cook with the lid on, top vent half open, for 1 hour 10 minutes, or until golden and cooked through (the internal temperature of the breast should be at least 160°F), turning breast side up halfway through. When you turn it, halve and add the lemon to the grate cut side down, and baste the chicken with olive oil using the herbs as a brush, if you like.

4 Spread the reserved sauce onto a serving platter, place the chicken on top and let it rest for 30 minutes – the internal temperature needs to reach 165°F in the breast and 175°F in the thigh.

5 Holding the remaining pomegranate half cut side down in the palm of your hand, bash the back with a spoon so all the seeds tumble out over the chicken, then squeeze on the charred lemon juice. Great served with Crispy chickpea hummus (page 214) or Squash, sage & rice salad (page 102).

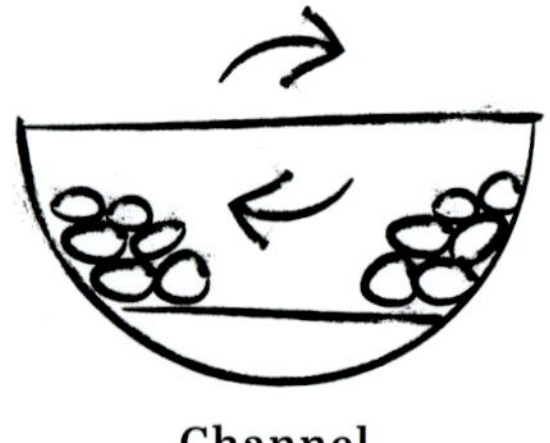

Channel

Rôtisserie it up! If you have a motorized rôtisserie kit and the means to build a firepit, I'd recommend it! Set up hot and medium zones and get the rôtisserie ready in line with the medium part. Carefully thread the chicken onto the rôtisserie skewer, with a lemon half at each end. Set it into the rôtisserie about 16 inches from the medium coals (and no higher than 24 inches). Cook as above, keeping the fire as even as possible.

Ultimate pork ribs 3 ways

Serves 6–8 | 2 hours 30 minutes, plus resting

3 lbs baby back ribs

⅓ x Bay salt (page 218)

4 tablespoons unsalted butter

scant ¼ cup apple cider

½ an orange

Choose your glaze:

BBQ sauce

½ x Pantry BBQ sauce (page 202)

Hoisin

¾ cup hoisin sauce

1 orange

Mango chutney

½ a pomegranate

1 jar of mango chutney

1 Light the grill (pages 16–19). Soak a handful of wood chips according to the package instructions. Rub the Bay salt (page 218) all over the ribs and place on the cool zone. Drain the wood chips and place them on the hot zone. Cook with the lid on, top vent half open, for 1 hour, or until golden, turning halfway.

2 Lay out a double layer of heavy-duty aluminum foil (12 inches long) and top with a sheet of parchment paper. Place 1 rack of ribs in the center, dot with butter, drizzle with cider, then place the other rack(s) on top and repeat. Slice and add the orange. Fold in the foil overhang, tightly rolling in the sides to seal. Return to the cool zone and cook lid on, top vent half open, for 1 hour.

3 Meanwhile, make your chosen glaze. Whip up a batch of Pantry BBQ sauce (page 202), mix the hoisin with the orange juice until smooth, or squeeze the pomegranate juice into a bowl and mix with the mango chutney.

4 Unwrap the ribs and check the meat is soft and tender, then carefully pour any cooking juices into your glaze. Transfer the ribs to the medium-hot zone in a single layer and use a pastry brush or the back of a spoon to glaze them all over. Cook lid on, top vent open, for 5 to 10 minutes, or until the glaze sets, basting occasionally (the temperature will be low, so if you've got guests coming round, it will hold the ribs beautifully until you're ready to dish up!).

5 Serve the ribs on a big board or platter with garnishes of your choice or like you see in the picture, slice up and dig in!

Ingredient know-how: You can ask your butcher to remove the membrane on the underside of the ribs, or use a narrow, sharp knife to do it yourself – I personally like it, though, for a bit of added flavor and texture.

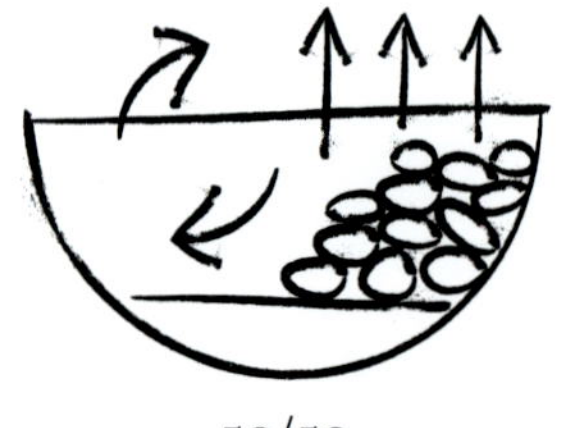

50/50

Buddy's chicken Caesar

Serves 6–8 | 1 hour 30 minutes, plus resting

- 1 bunch of mixed woody herbs (about ⅔ oz) such as rosemary, thyme
- 1 x 4½-lb whole chicken
- 3 lemons
- 4 x 1-inch-thick slices of sourdough bread
- 1 sweetheart or green cabbage
- 4 mixed-color chilies
- 1 x 2-oz tin of anchovy fillets
- ½ teaspoon dried oregano
- 1 clove of garlic
- 1 heaping teaspoon English or Dijon mustard
- 2 tablespoons Worcestershire sauce
- ⅓ cup Greek yogurt
- 2 oz Parmesan cheese
- 1 bunch broccolini (8 oz)
- 12 slices of bacon
- 2 heads of romaine lettuce

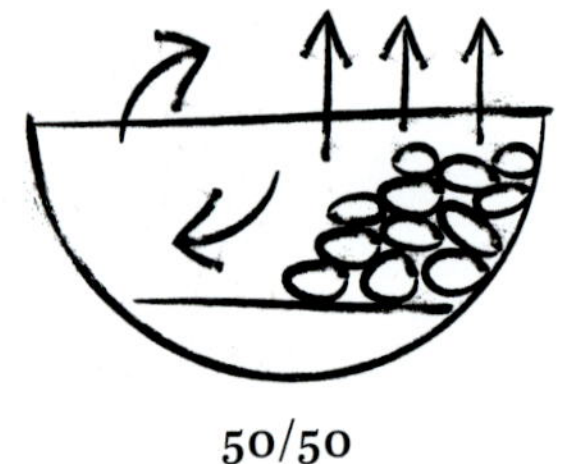

50/50

1 Light the grill (pages 16–19). Soak a handful of wood chips according to the package instructions. Strip half the herb leaves into a mortar and pestle, pound with a pinch each of sea salt and black pepper, then muddle in 2 tablespoons of olive oil. Use a large sharp knife to carefully cut down one side of the chicken's backbone, so you can open it out flat. Rub it all over with the herby oil, then place skin side down on the hot zone to sear for 5 minutes, flipping halfway. Halve and char 2 lemons alongside. Put the bread on the cool zone.

2 Drain the wood chips and place on the hot zone with half the remaining herb sprigs for bonus fragrance. Place the chicken on top of the bread with the legs toward the medium zone and sprinkle on the last of the herbs. Place the cabbage on the hot zone. Prick the chilies and place on the medium-cool zone. Cook with the lid on, top vent half open, for 1 hour, or until the internal temperature of the chicken breast is at least 160°F, spritzing with oil occasionally, and removing the lemons and chilies after 20 minutes.

3 Once cool enough to handle, scrape the blackened skin off the chilies, discard the seeds and stems, then slice lengthwise and lay on a plate with the anchovies. Squeeze on half the fresh lemon juice, sprinkle with the dried oregano, add a few drops of extra virgin olive oil, and set aside.

4 For the dressing, bash the garlic into a paste in a mortar and pestle. Mix in the mustard, Worcestershire sauce and yogurt. Finely grate in the Parmesan, squeeze in 3 of the charred lemon halves, then finely chop and add one of them, along with a drizzle of oil from the anchovy tin. Season to perfection.

5 Transfer the chicken and bread to a board and let the chicken rest for 30 minutes – the internal temperature needs to reach 165°F in the breast and 175°F in the thigh. Trim the broccolini, halving any thicker stems lengthwise. Lay the bacon on the hot zone, scatter the broccolini on top and cook lid on, top vent half open, for 10 to 15 minutes, removing once golden.

6 Tear up the toasts. Separate out the lettuce leaves. Trim the cabbage, discard the outer burnt layers and roughly slice. Toss it all with the dressing, bacon and broccolini. Serve with the golden chicken and anchovies.

Veggie gumbo

Serves 6–8 | 1 hour 10 minutes

3 heaping tablespoons all-purpose flour

1 onion

4 green bell peppers

4 jalapeños

2 cloves of garlic

3 stalks of celery

2 ears of corn, husked

8 oz okra

4 scallions

2 tablespoons Old Bay seasoning

1½ x 13-oz jars of chickpeas

1 x 14.5-oz can of whole tomatoes

4 cups (1 quart) veg stock

4 sprigs of Italian parsley

I've been lucky enough to taste some truly incredible gumbos with the good people of New Orleans, and this veggie version is inspired by those epic dishes.

1 Light the grill (pages 16–19). Add 3 tablespoons of olive oil to a large shallow Dutch oven on the medium-hot zone and stir in the flour to make a paste. Cook until dark brown, stirring constantly. Meanwhile, halve the unpeeled onion, prick the peppers and jalapeños, then char on the hot zone with the unpeeled garlic, the celery, corn, okra and scallions for 15 minutes, turning regularly and moving to the cool zone if coloring too quickly. Transfer to your board once charred. You may need to work in batches.

2 Once cool enough to handle, peel and finely chop the onion and garlic, and add to the pan along with the Old Bay. Cook for 5 minutes, or until softened and dark nutty brown, stirring regularly.

3 Scrape the blackened skin off the peppers, discard the seeds and stems, then chop up with the celery and okra. Use a large sharp knife to cut the corn kernels off the cobs, discarding the cobs, and add it all to the pan along with the chickpeas, juices and all. Pour in the tomatoes, breaking them up with your spoon, add the veg stock, then carefully move the pan to the cool zone. Cook with the lid on, vents open, for 45 minutes, or until the veg is tender and the stew is gloriously thick.

4 Meanwhile, trim and roughly chop the charred scallions and jalapeños, discarding the stems, then mix with 1 tablespoon of red wine vinegar and a pinch of sea salt, and set aside to quickly pickle.

5 Season the stew to perfection, spoon on the pickled veg, pick and sprinkle on the parsley leaves and serve. Great with a pan of hot fluffy rice.

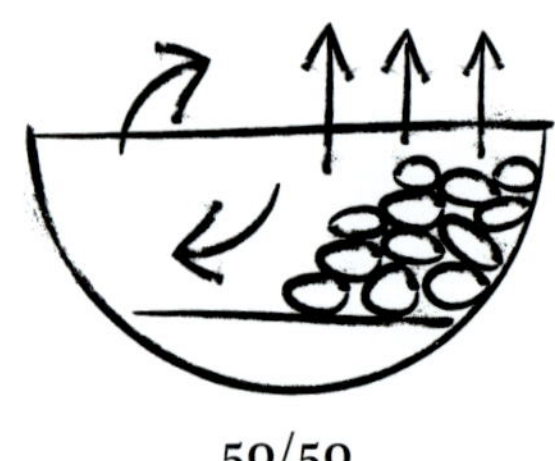

50/50

Fruity pork chops & grilled potatoes

Serves 6–8 | 1 hour

2 lbs new potatoes

1 bunch of scallions

1¾ lbs stone fruit, such as plums, peaches, apricots

1 bunch of sage (about ⅔ oz)

4 cloves of garlic

2 fresh bay leaves

⅔ cup whisky

1 tablespoon runny honey

4 x 14- to 16-oz thick center-cut pork loin chops, bone in

1 Light the grill (pages 16–19). Slice the potatoes a scant ½ inch thick and set aside. Trim and halve the scallions. Halve and pit the stone fruit. Grill the scallions and fruit on the medium-hot zone until marked, turning regularly with tongs and moving to the cool zone if coloring too quickly.

2 Put a large shallow Dutch oven on the cool zone and add 1 tablespoon of olive oil. Pick in the sage leaves and, once they start to crisp up, add the grilled scallions. Peel, slice and add the garlic, along with the bay leaves. Add the grilled stone fruit to the pan as it's done.

3 Pour in the whisky and carefully flame it, if you like (stand back!), then add the honey and a pinch each of sea salt and black pepper. Carefully move the pan to the hot zone and let it all reduce for 10 minutes, or until soft, sticky and the fruit has started to break down, adding splashes of water to keep it syrupy. Remove the pan from the grill and transfer to a heatproof surface.

4 Score into the fat on the pork chops at ½-inch intervals, ¼ inch deep. Season with salt, spritz with olive oil, then grill for 5 to 10 minutes on the hot or medium zone, turning halfway and moving to the cooler zone if your coals flare up. Transfer the chops to the pan and carefully move it back to the cool zone so the chops can cook through for 5 more minutes. Remove, cover and let rest.

5 Use tongs to lay the potato slices on the hot zone, and cook with the lid on, vents open, for 5 minutes, or until marked, then move to the medium-cool zone, lid on, vents open, for another 10 to 15 minutes, or until cooked through, turning regularly and spritzing with oil. Dish it all up together, slicing the pork to serve. Great with a simple green salad.

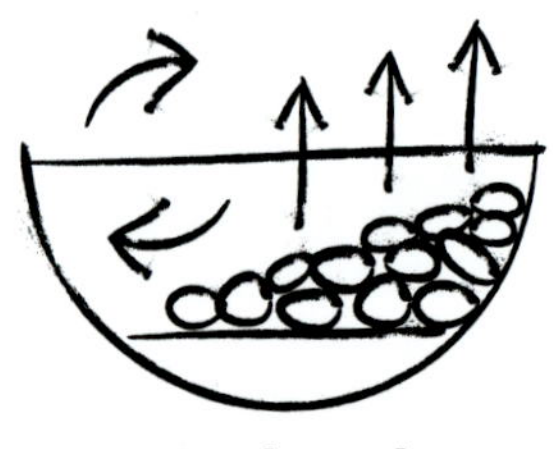

Graduated

Super surf & turf mixed grill

Serves 4 | 45 minutes

2 scallions

2 cloves of garlic

2 lemons

1 teaspoon drained capers

1 x 2-oz tin of anchovy fillets

½ a bunch of mixed soft herbs (about ½ oz)

1 cup (2 sticks) softened unsalted butter

½ a bulb of fennel

6 oz green beans

½ a sourdough or French baguette

4 small bone-in, skin-on chicken thighs (1 lb total)

4 oz cured chorizo

8 raw shell-on jumbo shrimp

1¼ lbs mixed mussels & clams, scrubbed, debearded

1 cup ripe cherry tomatoes

¼ cup dry white wine

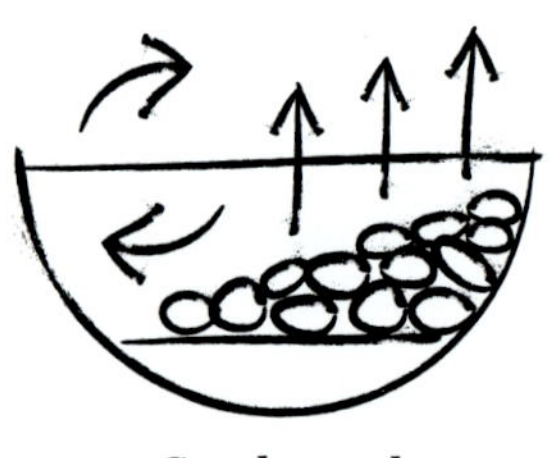

Graduated

1 To make a flavored butter, trim and roughly chop the scallions, peel the garlic and finely grate the zest of 1 lemon, then blitz it all in a food processor with the capers, anchovies and most of the soft herb leaves (or chop by hand on a board). Blitz or mix in the softened butter until combined.

2 Trim the fennel and cut into thin wedges, trim the green beans and slice the baguette on the bias. Rub the chicken with 2 tablespoons of olive oil and season with sea salt and black pepper. Slice the chorizo a scant ½ inch thick. Peel the shrimp, leaving the tails on, then run a small sharp knife down the back of each, discarding the vein. Check the mussels and clams, tapping any open ones, and if they don't close, discard. Light the grill (pages 16–19).

3 Place the chicken skin side down in a large shallow cast-iron pan on the hot zone, then add the chorizo and cook with the grill lid on, vents open, for 10 minutes, or until the fat has rendered out and the skin is crisp. Flip the chicken over and place it directly on the medium zone to cook lid on, vents open, for 10 minutes, or until cooked through (the internal temp should be 170°F), turning regularly, then transfer to a serving platter with the chorizo.

4 Cook the fennel in the rendered fat in the pan for 5 minutes, then add the green beans for 2 more minutes, turning until golden. Transfer the beans to the platter, and the fennel to the cool zone. Cook the tomatoes in the pan for 2 minutes, or until blistered. Toast the bread in the pan at the same time, turning and spritzing with olive oil, as needed, then arrange it all on the platter.

5 Add the mussels, clams and shrimp to the pan. Pour in the wine and add 3 tablespoons of flavored butter. Cook lid on, vents open, for 5 minutes, or until the clams and mussels have opened (discard any that remain closed) and the shrimp are cooked through, then transfer to the platter with the fennel. Spoon on the lovely hot pan juices, pick and sprinkle on the remaining herbs, and serve with lemon wedges. The leftover flavored butter will keep for up to 2 weeks in the fridge, or up to 3 months in the freezer. Fast future flavor awaits!

Duck legs & plum sauce

Serves 4 | Prep 10 minutes | Cook 2 hours

4 teaspoons Bay salt (page 218)

4 duck legs

8 plums

1 bunch of woody herbs (about ⅔ oz), such as bay, thyme, oregano, rosemary

1 sweetheart or green cabbage

1½ cups whole grain basmati rice

6 fresh bay leaves

1½ x 13-oz jars of chickpeas

¼ cup Greek yogurt

1 Light the grill (pages 16–19). Place a roasting pan with 2 cups of water underneath the grate in the cool zone – this will help the duck legs steam and you'll also capture the lovely juices in the pan as they cook.

2 Rub the Bay salt (page 218) all over the duck legs, then place them on the hot zone for 5 minutes, or until golden all over, turning regularly. Move to the cool zone over the pan and cook with the lid on, vents open, for 1 hour.

3 When the time's up, line up the plums next to the duck on the cool zone. Place the bunch of herbs on the hot zone, place the cabbage on top, and cook it all with the lid on, vents open, for another 1 hour, or until the duck meat pulls away from the bone, topping up the tray with more water if it looks dry (don't be alarmed when the cabbage and herbs blacken – they're meant to!).

4 With 35 minutes to go, add the rice, bay and a small pinch of sea salt to a cast-iron pan with 2 cups of boiling water and the chickpeas, juices and all. Place on the medium zone and cook lid on, vents open, for 30 minutes, then carefully remove the pan from the grill, cover and steam for 5 minutes.

5 Mash the plums in a shallow serving bowl, discarding the pits, then lay the duck legs on top. Trim the cabbage, removing the burnt outer layers, then thickly slice. Mix up the rice and chickpeas, season to perfection, and dish it all up together, rippling the plum sauce with the yogurt, to serve.

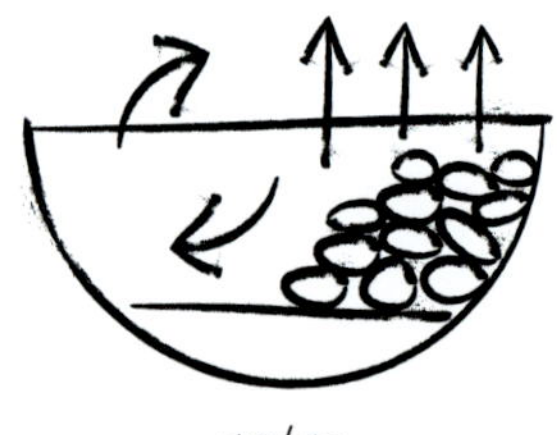

50/50

Veg-tastic barbecue mezze

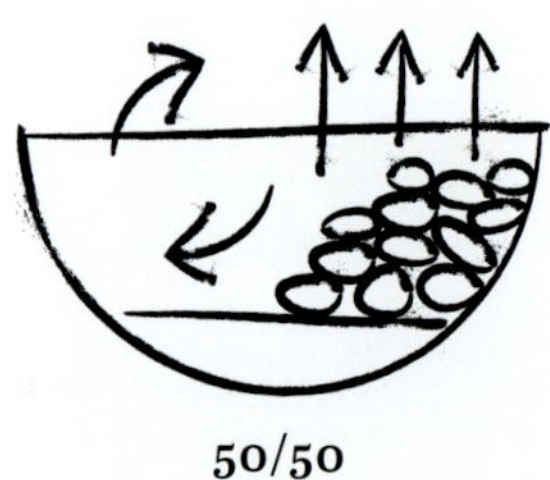

50/50

Mighty veg do wonderful things when grilled, blackened, charred and blistered – there are so many ways to create big flavor. I'm sharing a few of my favorites here, and the recipes on these pages make a spectacular spread when all cooked together. Plus, I've added a couple of supplementary dishes that really finish off the party – namely a beautiful labneh, easy sesame flatbread and a flavor-boosted tin of anchovies. Feel free to pick and choose the elements that make your heart sing, or go all out and cook everything up for a veg-tastic feast.

Mint & chili zucchini

Serves 6 | 25 minutes

Light the grill (pages 16–19). Place **2 zucchini** on the hot zone and cook with the lid on, vents open, for 20 minutes, or until charred, turning occasionally. Roughly chop, scrape into a bowl, then chop and add the leaves from **a few sprigs of mint**. Thinly slice and add **1 fresh red chili**, then mix with ½ tablespoon of red wine vinegar and 1 tablespoon of extra virgin olive oil and season to perfection.

Burnt butter labneh

Serves 6 | 10 minutes, plus draining

Light the grill (pages 16–19). Place a sieve over a bowl and line with a few layers of paper towels. Add **2 heaping cups of Greek yogurt** and a pinch of sea salt, then pull up the paper towels around the yogurt and very gently apply pressure so that the liquid starts to drip through into the bowl. Let drain in the fridge until it becomes the consistency of cream cheese. Gently squeeze out and discard any remaining liquid, then transfer to a serving bowl. Finely grate in the zest of **1 lemon**, squeeze in the juice and mix to make labneh. Melt **4 tablespoons of unsalted butter** in a cast-iron pan on the medium zone until browned (or in a pan over medium heat on the stove), then stir in **2 tablespoons of dukkah** and pour over the labneh. Nice topped with a few **thyme tips**, if you have them.

Anchovies & orange

Serves 6 | 3 minutes

Take **1 x 2-oz tin of anchovy fillets in oil**, squeeze in the juice from **½ an orange**, then finely chop and add **a few soft herbs, like parsley or mint leaves, or fennel fronds**.

Halloumi & apricots

Serves 6 | 25 minutes

Light the grill (pages 16–19). Pat dry, then lightly score an **8-oz block of halloumi**, drizzle with 1 tablespoon of olive oil and cook on the hot zone for 10 minutes, or until soft, golden and marked, turning halfway. Cook **6 whole ripe apricots** alongside until beautifully charred, turning occasionally, then, once cool enough to handle, tear into an ovenproof dish, discarding the pits. Place the halloumi on top, then pick and sprinkle on a few **thyme leaves**. Drizzle with 1 tablespoon of oil and **1 teaspoon of runny honey**, if you like, and return to the cool zone for a few extra minutes, or until bubbling.

Baba ganoush

Serves 6 | 25 minutes

Light the grill (pages 16–19). Prick **2 small eggplants (8 oz each)**, place on the hot zone and cook with the lid on, vents open, for 20 minutes, or until soft and blackened, turning occasionally, then remove (or cook the eggplants directly on the coals, if you prefer). Slice them open and scoop the flesh into a bowl. Add **2 tablespoons of tahini** and the juice of **1 lemon**, finely grate in **½ a clove of garlic**, trim, thinly slice and add **2 scallions**, then finely chop and add **½ a bunch of Italian parsley (about ½ oz)**, stems and all. Roughly mash, season to perfection, and finish with a drizzle of extra virgin olive oil.

Sweet peppers & capers

Serves 6 | 25 minutes

Light the grill (pages 16–19). Prick **2 mixed-color bell peppers**, place on the hot zone and cook with the lid on, vents open, for 20 minutes, or until blackened, turning occasionally and adding **6 pricked padrón peppers** for the final 5 minutes. Once cool enough to handle, remove the skins from just the mixed-color bell peppers, then thinly slice all the peppers into long strips and add to a bowl, discarding the seeds and stems. Pit and tear on **5 olives**, then squeeze on and add **1 tablespoon drained capers** and sprinkle with a little red wine vinegar. Use a vegetable peeler to remove the peel of **½ a lemon**, slice into very thin strips and scatter on, then finish with a drizzle of extra virgin olive oil, if you like.

Tear & share flatbread

Serves 6 | 8 minutes, plus resting

You need an even heat to cook this bread, so carefully shake out your hot coals to evenly cover the bottom of the grill. In a bowl, mix **2 cups of self-rising flour** (see note on page 84) with a pinch of sea salt, **1¼ cups of plain yogurt** and 2 tablespoons of olive oil until you have a dough, then cover and let rest for at least 15 minutes. Sprinkle **2 tablespoons of sesame seeds** over the dough and roll out on a floured surface into one large flatbread that's just over ⅛ inch thick. Use the rolling pin to gently roll it up, then unroll it onto the grill and cook for 3 minutes, or until golden, turning halfway.

Paprika pulled pork

Serves 10 | 2 hours 15 minutes, plus resting

4½-lb piece of boneless, skinless pork shoulder

1 tablespoon smoked paprika

1 Light the grill (pages 16–19) and soak a handful of wood chips according to the package instructions, if you like. Place a roasting pan with 2 cups of water underneath the grate in the cool zone – this will help the pork steam and you'll also capture the lovely juices in the pan as it cooks.

2 Cut the pork into 4 equal chunks, drizzle with 1 tablespoon each of red wine vinegar and olive oil, then rub all over with the paprika and a big pinch each of sea salt and black pepper. Sear on the hot zone for 10 minutes, turning regularly and moving to the medium or cool zone if coloring too quickly.

3 Once seared, move the pork chunks to the cool zone above the pan of water and cook with the lid on, top vent half open, for 2 hours, or until the pork is gnarly and shreds easily with a dark bark, turning occasionally. Rest the pork for 30 minutes, loosely covered with aluminum foil.

4 Carefully skim away most of the fat from the juices in the pan. Shred and pull apart the meat with two forks, discarding any gristly bits, then add the meat to the pan and toss with the juices. Great served with a simple slaw and a stack of soft brioche buns (or make your own buns, page 224), as well as mustard, or your favorite condiments like Pantry BBQ sauce (page 202), Chili sauce (page 204), or my Smoky ketchup (page 212).

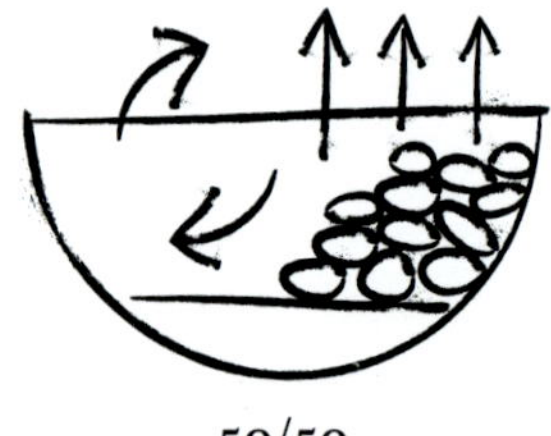

50/50

Burgers & patties

Gravy cheeseburgers

Serves 4 | 25 minutes

1 lb ground beef (20% fat)

¼ of an English cucumber

1 large ripe tomato

1 red onion

½ teaspoon jarred horseradish

½ a bunch of Italian parsley (about ½ oz)

2 slices of bacon

1 teaspoon Marmite

2 tablespoons all-purpose flour

2 cups beef stock

2 teaspoons English or Dijon mustard

⅓ cup mayo (or make your own, page 210)

4 burger buns (or make your own, page 224)

4 slices of Cheddar cheese (about 2 oz)

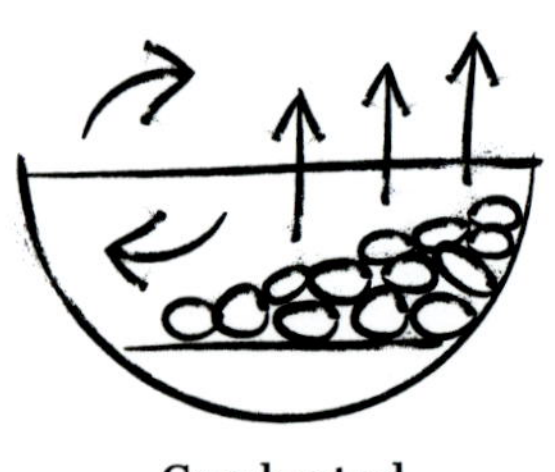

Graduated

1 Divide the meat equally into four and shape into patties just under ½ inch thick. Season well with sea salt and black pepper.

2 Slice the cucumber on the bias. Slice the tomato ¼ inch thick. Peel and very thinly slice most of the onion into rounds, reserving a third. Add it all to a bowl, season with salt, add 1 tablespoon of red wine vinegar and the horseradish, then scrunch together well. Drizzle with 1 tablespoon of extra virgin olive oil, and pick and add the parsley.

3 Finely chop the reserved onion third, thinly slice the bacon, then cook in a frying pan over medium-high heat on the stove with a drizzle of olive oil for 5 minutes, or until the onion is softened and the bacon is golden. Stir in the Marmite, then the flour for 1 minute. Gradually stir in the stock, simmer for a few minutes, or until thickened, then season to perfection with black pepper.

4 Mix the mustard into the mayo. Halve the buns. Light the grill (pages 16–19). Cook the burgers on the hot zone for 3 to 4 minutes on each side, moving to the medium zone if they're coloring too quickly, then lay on the cheese, put the lid on, vents open, and let the cheese melt for a minute, toasting the buns alongside. Reheat the gravy, if needed.

5 In the buns, layer up the mustard mayo, quick-pickled veg and burgers in whatever way makes you happy, squash together, dunk in the gravy, and devour! Serve the extra pickled veg on the side.

Miso mushroom burgers

Serves 4 | 25 minutes

2 tablespoons miso

2 tablespoons mirin

1 tablespoon reduced-sodium soy sauce

1 tablespoon maple syrup

1 large ripe avocado

2 limes

¼ a small head of green cabbage (6 oz)

½ an English cucumber (6 oz)

4 large portobello mushrooms

1 bunch of scallions

4 burger buns (or make your own, page 224)

1 To make the glaze, mix the miso with 1 tablespoon of mirin, the soy and maple until combined. Halve and pit the avo, scoop the flesh into a bowl, mash with the remaining mirin and the juice of ½ a lime, and season to perfection. Use a vegetable peeler to thinly shred the cabbage, then dress with the juice of 1 lime and a pinch each of sea salt and black pepper. Use the peeler to shave the cucumber into ribbons. Light the grill (pages 16–19).

2 Trim the mushroom stems, then grill the mushrooms on the hot zone, lid on, vents open, for 2 minutes, turning halfway. Move them to the cool zone and cook for another 6 minutes, turning every minute and brushing with the glaze on each turn. Char the scallions alongside, then transfer to your board, trim, chop and mix with the cabbage. Halve and toast the buns.

3 Spread the bun bottoms with avo, layer up with some cabbage and scallions, the mushrooms and some cucumber ribbons, spread any leftover glaze on the bun tops, then squash together, serving the remaining veg on the side.

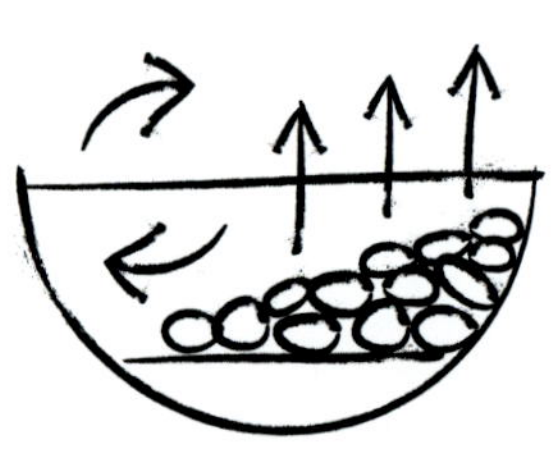

Graduated

Lamb moussaka burgers

Serves 4 | 30 minutes

8 oz feta cheese

1 lb ground lamb (20% fat)

½ teaspoon ground cumin

4 burger buns (or make your own, page 224)

1 small eggplant (8 oz)

12 oz ripe tomatoes on the vine

4 scallions

1 bunch of Italian parsley (about 1 oz)

1 Blitz the feta in a small blender or food processor with ½ cup of water until smooth, thinning with extra splashes of water, if needed, until drizzleable. Pour half into a bowl, stashing the rest in the fridge, where it will keep happily for up to 3 days. Light the grill (pages 16–19).

2 Divide the meat equally into four and shape into scant ½-inch-thick patties. Sprinkle the cumin on a plate with a pinch each of sea salt and black pepper, then turn the burgers in the seasoning to coat both sides. Halve the buns.

3 Slice the eggplant lengthwise a scant ½ inch thick. Place on the hot zone with the vine of tomatoes and the whole scallions, turning regularly, and transferring to a board when soft and charred. Trim the scallions, then finely chop with the eggplant and tomatoes, discarding the tomato vine. Mix with 1 tablespoon of red wine vinegar and season to perfection. Pick the parsley leaves and dress with a little extra virgin olive oil.

4 Cook the lamb burgers on the hot zone for 2 minutes on each side, or until cooked through, moving to the medium zone if they're coloring too quickly, and toasting the buns alongside.

5 Layer up the moussaka veg mixture, the burgers and blitzed feta, pile the dressed parsley on top, put the bun tops on, and enjoy!

Leftover love: Leftover blitzed feta is delicious drizzled over grilled veg, salad or eggs, or used to dress beans or chickpeas.

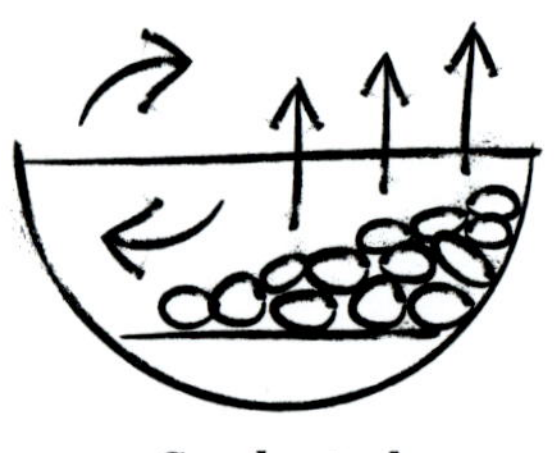

Graduated

Sesame chicken burgers

Serves 4 | 30 minutes

1 lime

1 tablespoon gochujang paste

¼ cup Greek yogurt, plus extra to serve

1 red bell pepper

4 scallions

¼ a small head of green cabbage (6 oz)

½ an English cucumber

2 sprigs of mint

4 burger buns (or make your own, page 224)

2 tablespoons sesame seeds

1 lb ground chicken (20% fat)

1 Light the grill (pages 16–19). Finely grate and reserve the lime zest. In a little bowl, mix the gochujang and yogurt with a squeeze of lime juice until smooth, then season with sea salt. Seed and very thinly slice the pepper, trim and thinly slice the scallions, very thinly shred the cabbage, score the skin of the cucumber with a fork to create grooves, then thinly slice into rounds. Thinly slice the mint leaves. Dress it all with the remaining lime juice and 1 tablespoon of extra virgin olive oil, scrunch well, and season to perfection.

2 Spread the sesame seeds on a small plate. Season the chicken well with salt and black pepper, then scrunch with the reserved lime zest. Divide the chicken mixture equally into four and shape into ¾-inch-thick patties, dipping into the sesame seeds to coat all over. Halve the buns.

3 Spritz the burgers with olive oil and cook on the hot zone for 6 minutes on each side, or until golden and cooked through, moving to the medium zone if they're coloring too quickly, and toasting the buns alongside.

4 Layer up the gochujang yogurt, quick-pickled veg and burgers. Spoon on more yogurt, and get the tops on, serving the remaining veg on the side.

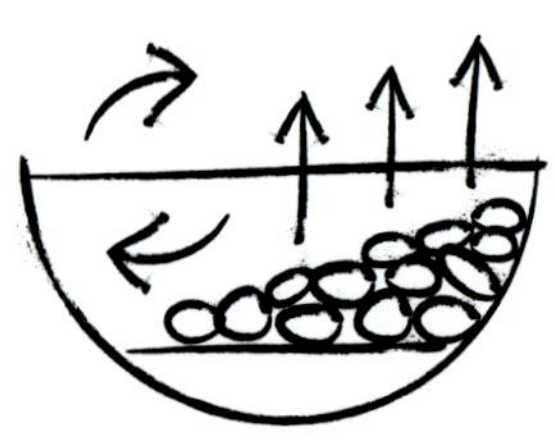

Graduated

Blue cheese pork burgers

Serves 4 | **20 minutes**

½ a bunch of chives (about ⅓ oz)

8 cornichons

1 small apple

1 lemon

1 heaping teaspoon Dijon mustard

1 little gem lettuce

1 handful of mâche or baby spinach

½ cup shelled walnut halves

1 lb ground pork

4 burger buns (or make your own, page 224)

4 oz Stilton cheese

3 tablespoons crème fraîche

1 For a delicate salsa, finely chop the chives and thinly slice the cornichons. Very finely dice the apple. Squeeze on half the lemon juice, mix and set aside.

2 To make a French dressing, whisk the mustard, remaining lemon juice and 3 tablespoons of extra virgin olive oil in a bowl, then season to perfection with sea salt. Reserve 1 tablespoon of dressing, then separate out the gem leaves and add to the bowl with the mâche, ready to toss at the last minute.

3 For the patties, crush the walnuts, then mix into the pork with a pinch each of salt and black pepper. Divide equally into four, shape into scant ½-inch-thick patties and spritz with olive oil. Light the grill (pages 16–19).

4 Sear the burgers on the hot zone for 90 seconds on each side, then brush with the reserved French dressing and cook for another 3 minutes on each side, or until golden and cooked through, brushing with more dressing when you turn them and moving to the medium zone if they're coloring too quickly. Toast the buns alongside. Crumble the Stilton into a small enamel dish, add the crème fraîche and melt on the cool zone, stirring occasionally, then remove.

5 Layer up the oozy cheese, dressed leaves, burgers and salsa on the buns. Serve with the extra dressed leaves and oozy cheese on the side, for dunking.

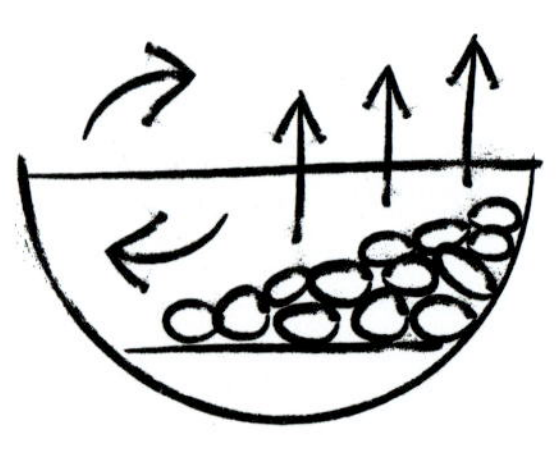

Graduated

Beet & feta bean burgers

Serves 4 | 25 minutes, plus chilling

2 red onions

1 cup frozen shelled fava beans or shelled edamame

1 x 15-oz can of chickpeas

1 x 8.5-oz package of cooked mixed quinoa

1 heaping teaspoon ground cumin

1 heaping teaspoon smoked paprika

6 oz vacuum-packed beets

4 burger buns (or make your own, page 224)

½ a bunch of soft herbs (about ½ oz), such as mint, Italian parsley

¼ cup plain yogurt

2 oz feta cheese

1 Peel 1 onion, then quarter it and break into petals. Cook in a large, dry frying pan over high heat on the stove with the frozen fava beans for 5 minutes, or until charred and softened, tossing regularly, then transfer it all to a food processor (of course, if you have the grill lit for other things, you could char it all in a metal sieve over the grate instead).

2 Drain the chickpeas and add to the processor with the quinoa, spices, 1 teaspoon of red wine vinegar and a pinch each of sea salt and black pepper. Blitz until finely chopped and combined, stopping to scrape down the sides, as needed. Use clean, wet hands to divide and shape the mixture into 4 patties about 1 inch thick. Rub with olive oil, then chill in the fridge until needed.

3 Peel and very thinly slice the remaining onion, then, in a bowl, scrunch with 1 tablespoon of red wine vinegar and a pinch of salt, and set aside to quickly pickle. Light the grill (pages 16–19).

4 Cook the burgers on the hot zone for 5 minutes, or until nicely charred, turning halfway, then move to the medium-cool zone and cook for another 5 minutes with the lid on, vents open, or until cooked through. Pat the beets dry with paper towels and char alongside the burgers for the last 5 minutes, turning occasionally. Halve and toast the buns.

5 Remove and thinly slice the beets. Pick the herbs. Spread the bun bottoms with the yogurt, add the burgers, beets, pickled red onion, herb leaves and a crumbling of feta, then pop the tops on and enjoy!

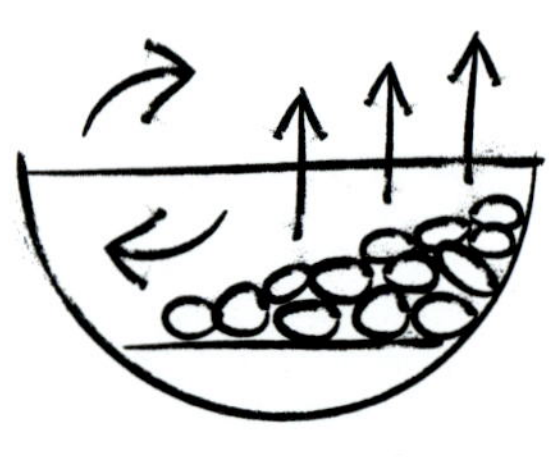

Graduated

Shrimp toast burgers

Serves 4 as a main / 8 as a side | 20 minutes

1 English cucumber

1 fresh red chili

2 limes

2 tablespoons chili jam

2 tablespoons Greek yogurt

4-inch piece of ginger

2 scallions

1 lb peeled raw extra-large shrimp, tails removed

1 teaspoon English or Dijon mustard

¼ cup sesame seeds, a mix of black and white

4 burger buns (or make your own, page 224)

2 sprigs of cilantro

1 Roughly peel the cucumber to make it stripy, then thinly slice into rounds and add to a large bowl. Finely chop and add the chili, then finely grate in the zest of 1 lime and squeeze in the juice. Toss together and season to perfection. Mix the chili jam and yogurt together.

2 Peel the ginger, trim the scallions, then roughly chop and add to a food processor. Blitz until fairly fine, then pulse in the shrimp, mustard and a pinch each of sea salt and black pepper until just combined.

3 Spread the sesame seeds on a small plate. Halve the buns. Divide the shrimp mixture and spread over the eight bun halves, using the back of a spoon to spread to the edges. Light the grill (pages 16–19) and give the grate a really good brush to clean it – this will help prevent the burgers from sticking.

4 Dip the shrimp side of each bun half into the sesame seeds, spritz with olive oil, then grill on the hot zone, sesame side down, for 5 minutes, or until cooked through, moving to the medium zone if they're coloring too quickly, and toasting the other side of each bun for just the last 30 seconds.

5 To serve, layer up the shrimp toasts with pickled cucumber and chili yogurt, then pick and sprinkle on the cilantro leaves and serve with lime wedges.

Helpful hint: Try dividing the shrimp mixture among baguette rounds for canape-sized toasts for lots of lucky people!

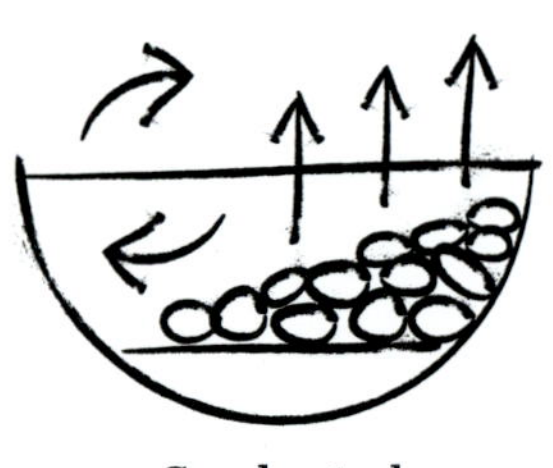

Graduated

Chorizo fish burgers

Serves 4 | **40 minutes**

2 red bell peppers

¼ cup slivered almonds

1 bunch of Italian parsley (about 1 oz)

2 oz Manchego cheese

2 lemons

4 burger buns (or make your own, page 224)

3 oz cured chorizo

1 lb firm white fish fillets, skin off, pin-boned

1 egg

1 Light the grill (pages 16–19) and give the grate a really good brush to clean it – this will help prevent the burgers from sticking. Prick the peppers and char on the hot zone, lid on, vents open, for 10 minutes.

2 Meanwhile, in a mortar and pestle, pound the almonds until fine. Pound in half the parsley leaves (reserving the stems) and finely grate in the cheese. Finely grate and reserve the lemon zest, then squeeze in the juice of 1 lemon and muddle in 2 tablespoons of extra virgin olive oil and a pinch of black pepper (do this in a food processor, if you prefer). Halve the buns.

3 Scrape off the larger bits of charred skin from the peppers, then cut them into strips, discarding the seeds and stems. Dress with ½ tablespoon of extra virgin olive oil and 1 teaspoon of red wine vinegar and set aside.

4 Thinly slice the parsley stems and finely chop the chorizo and half the fish, mixing it all with the reserved lemon zest as you go, until super-fine. Chop the rest of the fish into small chunks, then blend into the fine mixture. Scrunch in the egg, squashing and bringing it together well with clean hands.

5 Use the remaining parsley leaves to make 4 piles on your board the same diameter as your buns. Divide the burger mixture equally into four and, with wet hands, shape into balls, then flatten into 1-inch-thick patties on top of the piles of parsley, sticking the leaves to one side of each burger.

6 Cook the burgers, parsley side down, on the hot zone for 6 minutes, moving to the medium zone if they're coloring too quickly, then gently flip them over to cook for 2 minutes on the other side, or until cooked through. Thinly slice and grill the remaining lemon, toasting the buns alongside.

7 Spread the almond paste across the toasted bun bottoms, layer up the burgers, peppers and grilled lemon slices, pop the tops on and enjoy!

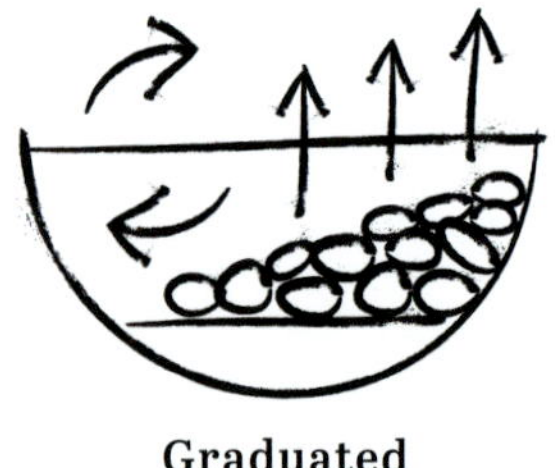

Graduated

Things that make the barbecue rock

Pantry BBQ sauce

Makes about 1¼ cups | 20 minutes, plus cooling

1 cinnamon stick

2 fresh bay leaves

1 lemon

1 clove of garlic

⅔ cup ketchup

¼ cup HP sauce

¼ cup Worcestershire sauce

2 tablespoons orange marmalade

1 teaspoon Marmite

2 teaspoons English or Dijon mustard

2 tablespoons honey or maple syrup

Pinch of ground ginger

scant ¼ cup port or red wine

1 If you've got the grill going, use a cast-iron pan on the hot zone, or, if you're cooking inside, use a small pan over high heat on the stove. Add 1 tablespoon of olive oil, the cinnamon and bay. Use a vegetable peeler to add a couple of strips of lemon peel, then smash and add the unpeeled garlic clove. Cook for 2 minutes, or until smelling fantastic, stirring regularly.

2 Stir in the ketchup, HP and Worcestershire sauces, marmalade, Marmite, mustard, honey, and ginger. Pour in the port, bring to a boil, then cover (lid on, vents open, if using the grill), and simmer for about 10 minutes, or until thick, stirring occasionally. Remove and discard the cinnamon, bay, lemon peel and garlic, or pass through a coarse sieve, then season to perfection, if needed.

3 Let cool completely, then use right away, or store in the fridge in sealed sterilized jars or bottles for up to 6 weeks. Once opened, use within 1 week. Great with my Ultimate pork ribs (page 158), Grilled fries (page 222) or Ultimate barbecue brekkie (pages 118–123).

Batch it up: This is a great recipe to double up so you have a good fridge stash, or to give away as gifts!

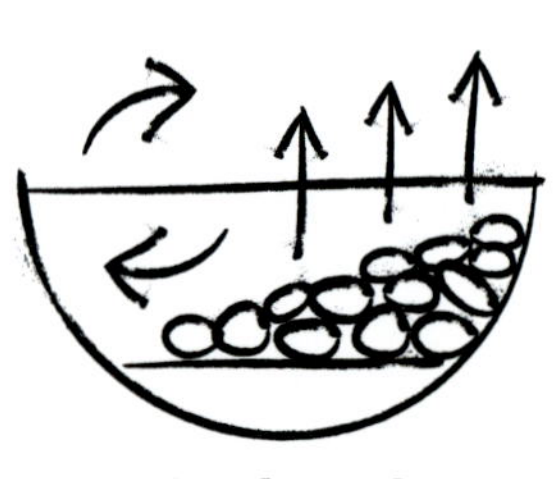

Graduated

Chili sauce

Makes about 2½ cups | 45 minutes, plus cooling

4 cloves of garlic

2 red bell peppers

10 fresh red chilies

2 teaspoons chili powder

1 lb ripe tomatoes

⅔ cup cider vinegar

3 tablespoons runny honey

1 cup unsweetened apple juice

You can buy some incredible chili sauces these days, and I have a whole range at home for different purposes. But when you have the time, you can't beat a batch of this homemade beauty! Double up, and make a friend happy, too.

1 Peel the garlic, seed the peppers and chilies, roughly chop and cook it all in a large shallow Dutch oven over medium heat on the stove with 2 tablespoons of olive oil for 10 minutes, or until softened, stirring regularly.

2 Stir in the chili powder, roughly chop and add the tomatoes, then the vinegar, honey, apple juice and ½ cup of water. Simmer for 30 minutes, or until reduced by half, stirring occasionally. Carefully transfer the mixture to a blender, add 2 teaspoons of sea salt and a pinch of black pepper, and blitz until smooth. You can leave the sauce as is, or you can pour it through a sieve to achieve a super-silky consistency. Either way, give it a taste, season to perfection, if needed, then cover and let cool completely.

3 Store in sealed sterilized jars or bottles in a cool, dark place for up to 6 weeks. Once opened, keep in the fridge and use within 3 days. Great with my Chicken shawarma (page 56) or Halloumi fritters (page 130).

Flavor boost: Seeding the chilies gives a medium heat, but feel free to leave the seeds in and go hotter, if you dare!

Salsa verde

Serves 8 | 10 minutes

½ a clove of garlic

1 x 2-oz tin of anchovy fillets in oil

5 cornichons

1 tablespoon drained capers

1 tablespoon Dijon mustard

1 bunch of Italian parsley (about 1 oz)

½ a bunch of basil (about ½ oz)

½ a bunch of mint (about ½ oz)

1 Peel the garlic, then very finely chop with the anchovies, cornichons and capers, mixing in the mustard to make a paste. Scrape into a bowl.

2 Pick, finely chop and add all the herb leaves. Stir in 1 tablespoon of red wine vinegar and 3 tablespoons of extra virgin olive oil, thinning with little splashes of water to a spoonable consistency. Season to perfection with sea salt and black pepper, and an extra splash of vinegar, to taste.

3 Delicious alongside my Classic leg of lamb (page 144) or Juicy pork belly, fennel & orange salad (page 136). Any leftovers can be stashed in the fridge, where they'll keep happily for up to 2 days.

Salsa rossa piccante

Serves 8 | 25 minutes

4 fresh red chilies

4 red or orange bell peppers

4 large ripe tomatoes

1 bulb of garlic

1 large red onion

1 teaspoon coriander seeds

1 cinnamon stick

1 lemon

1 bunch of Italian parsley (about 1 oz)

1 Light the grill (pages 16–19). Prick the chilies and peppers, then place whole on the hot zone with the tomatoes and the whole unpeeled garlic bulb. Halve and add the onion. Grill until charred and blackened all over, turning with tongs, and transferring it all to a large cold cast-iron pan when done. Put the lid on the pan and let everything steam for 10 minutes.

2 Meanwhile, in a mortar and pestle, pound the coriander seeds with 1 teaspoon each of sea salt and black pepper until fine.

3 Transfer all the veg to your board, and put the pan on the medium zone. Add 2 tablespoons of olive oil and the cinnamon. Peel or cut away and discard the charred parts of the red onion, then roughly chop and add to the pan. Squeeze the garlic cloves out of the skins, chop and add to the mix.

4 Peel off the blackened skin from the peppers, chilies and tomatoes, then roughly chop, removing the pepper and chili seeds and stems. Add it all to the pan – then, I like to scrape all the seeds and sludge from the board into a bowl and pass it through a sieve into the pan for maximum flavor. Add the coriander seasoning and cook for 10 minutes, stirring regularly, or until soft.

5 Remove from the heat, squeeze in the lemon juice, finely chop and add the parsley leaves and season to perfection. I like to keep it chunky, but you can finely chop it if you prefer. Great with meat, fish, halloumi, chunky veg and flatbreads or my Herby leg of lamb (page 152).

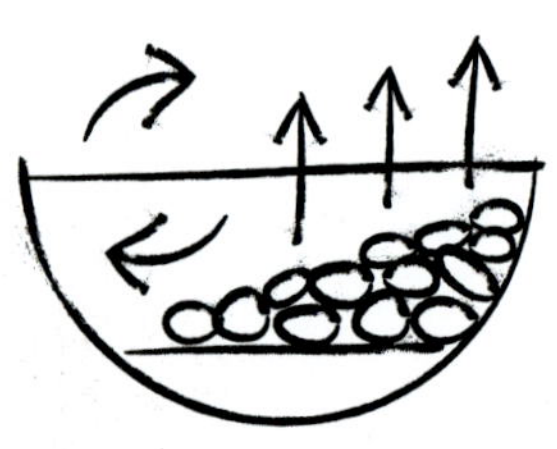

Graduated

Homemade mayo a multitude of ways

Makes 2 cups | **15 minutes**

1 large egg

1 teaspoon Dijon mustard

2 cups light olive oil

½ a lemon

In a large bowl, whisk the egg yolk (save the white for another day). Whisk in the mustard, then, whisking constantly, gradually add drops of the oil, moving to a light drizzle, and then a steady stream, and adding little splashes of red wine vinegar to thin, if it thickens too much. Season to perfection with sea salt, and a little lemon juice, if needed. It's great as it is, or you can add bonus flavor, as below. Either way, store any extra in a sterilized jar in the fridge for up to 1 week.

Basil mayo

In a mortar and pestle, pound the leaves from **½ a bunch of basil (about ½ oz)** into a paste, then muddle in **½ x Homemade mayo** until it's a beautiful pale green. Great with my Lemon steamed fish & charred greens (page 36).

Saffron mayo

Put **1 small pinch of saffron** into a small bowl with just **¼ of a teaspoon of boiling water** and let infuse for a few minutes. Muddle the saffron water into **½ x Homemade mayo**, until it becomes pale yellow. Lovely with my Sunshine stew & herb-stuffed sea bream (page 54)

Garlic mayo

Place **1 small bulb of garlic** underneath the grate next to the coals and let cook in its skin for 1 hour, or until charred but soft in the middle. Or, try throwing a handful of soaked wood chips on the dying embers and let the garlic smoke overnight with the lid on, top vent half open. Once cool enough to handle, squeeze out the soft flesh, discarding the skins, then mash and muddle into **½ x Homemade mayo**. Squeeze in a little **lemon juice**, to taste. Brilliant paired with my Skewered sardines on toast (page 68).

Curried mayo

Peel and finely grate **a scant ½ inch of ginger** into **½ x Homemade mayo**, then muddle in **½ a teaspoon of your favorite curry paste** and squeeze in a little **lemon juice**, to taste. Great with my Grilled fries (page 222).

Smoky ketchup

Makes 1½ cups | 45 minutes

1 fresh red chili

2 onions

1¾ lbs large ripe tomatoes

1 sprig of rosemary

2 cloves of garlic

1 x 16-oz jar of roasted red peppers

¼ cup packed light brown sugar

⅔ cup red wine vinegar

1 Light the grill (pages 16–19). Soak a handful of wood chips according to the package instructions.

2 Prick the chili, quarter the unpeeled onions, then place them all on the hot zone with the tomatoes. Grill until everything is charred and blackened all over, turning regularly with tongs, and transferring to a board once done.

3 Scrape the larger bits of blackened skin off the chili and tomatoes, seed the chili, then roughly chop both. Peel and roughly chop the onions. Scrape it all into a large cast-iron pan, add 2 tablespoons of olive oil, strip in the rosemary leaves, then peel, slice and add the garlic. Drain and add the peppers, add a pinch of black pepper and place the pan on the hot zone. Put the drained wood chips alongside, then cook with the grill lid on, vents open, for 15 minutes, or until softened.

4 Stir in the sugar, 1 teaspoon of sea salt and the vinegar and simmer for 5 minutes, then, in batches if needed, carefully blitz in a food processor until smooth. Pass through a sieve back into the pan, and simmer until thickened to the consistency of ketchup. Season to perfection, if needed.

5 Let cool completely, then use right away, or store in the fridge in sealed sterilized jars or bottles for up to 6 weeks. Once opened, use within 1 week.

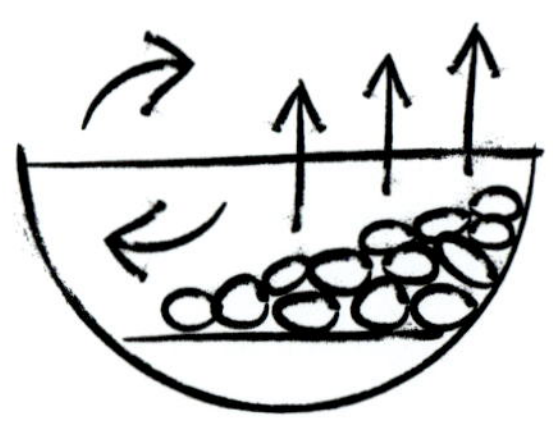

Graduated

Crispy chickpea hummus

Serves 10 | 15 minutes

- 1 tablespoon cumin seeds
- 1 x 24-oz jar of chickpeas, or 1½ x 15-oz cans of chickpeas
- 1 tablespoon sesame seeds
- 1 clove of garlic
- 2 tablespoons tahini
- 2 lemons
- 2 sprigs of thyme or oregano, flowering if you can get it
- 1 pinch of smoked paprika

1 Toast the cumin seeds in a frying pan over medium-high heat on the stove, or in a small enamel dish on the hot zone of the grill, if you've got it going. Once smelling fantastic, transfer half to a small bowl, and half to a blender.

2 Spritz the pan or dish with olive oil, then drain and pat dry ¼ cup of chickpeas and add in. Fry for 5 minutes, or until golden and crispy, adding the sesame seeds and the cumin from the bowl for the last minute.

3 Add the rest of the chickpeas, juices and all, to the blender. Peel and add the garlic, along with the tahini, 1 tablespoon of extra virgin olive oil, and a good pinch each of sea salt and black pepper. Squeeze in all the lemon juice, then blitz until silky and super-smooth. Taste and adjust the seasoning, if needed.

4 Spoon the hummus into a shallow serving bowl and make a well in the center. Top with the crispy chickpea mix, pick and sprinkle on the herbs, dust with the paprika, and finish with a drizzle of extra virgin olive oil, if you like.

Charred chili oil

Makes 1 small jar | 15 minutes, plus cooling

10 fresh mixed-color chilies

1 teaspoon dried oregano

½ cup extra virgin olive oil

When the grill's lit for a feast, this is one of those fantastic little bonus recipes I love to make on the side, utilizing that heat for mega flavor.

1 Light the grill (pages 16–19). Prick the chilies, then grill for 5 minutes, or until blackened and softened, turning regularly and transferring to a bowl once well charred. Cover, and let steam for 5 minutes.

2 Once cool enough to handle, scrape away and discard the chili skins, seeds and stems, then chop the soft flesh, mixing it with the oregano as you go.

3 Scrape the chili mixture into a clean jar, stir in 1 teaspoon each of sea salt and red wine vinegar, then top up with the oil and stash in the fridge for up to 4 weeks – the longer you leave it, the more the flavors develop. Great with grilled shrimp, steak or veggies, and a delight spooned over torn mozzarella on toast with a few fresh herbs and a grating of lemon zest.

Embellish it: I've kept it simple here, but you can absolutely make it your own by adding ingredients like toasted pine nuts, raisins or strips of lemon peel.

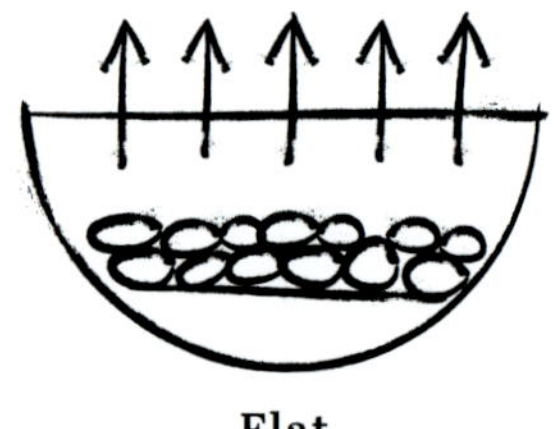

Flat

Bay salt

Makes 1 small jar | **10 minutes**

- 1 tablespoon coriander seeds
- 1 tablespoon fennel seeds
- 1 tablespoon granulated garlic
- 6 fresh bay leaves
- 1 lemon
- 1 pinch of dried red chili flakes

A wonderfully fragrant seasoning that can be used to add flavor to all sorts of different meats, fish or veggies prior to cooking or just before serving.

1. Blitz the coriander and fennel seeds, garlic and 1 tablespoon of black pepper in a blender until fine, or pound in a mortar and pestle.
2. Tear in the bay, discarding the stems, use a vegetable peeler to add the lemon peel in strips, add the chili flakes and 2 tablespoons of sea salt, then blitz again to incorporate, or pound well if using a mortar and pestle.
3. Use what you need right away in my Ultimate pork ribs (page 158) or Juicy pork belly, fennel & orange salad (page 136), or pop into a jar and store in a cool, dark place for up to 1 week.

Mega mac 'n' cheese

Serves 10 as a side | 1 hour

- 2 onions
- 2 cloves of garlic
- 2 tablespoons unsalted butter
- 2 fresh bay leaves
- ½ teaspoon cayenne pepper
- ⅓ cup all-purpose flour
- 5 cups reduced-fat milk
- 2 teaspoons English or Dijon mustard
- 1 lb elbow macaroni
- 8 oz aged Cheddar cheese, or a mix of Red Leicester and Cheddar, if you've got it
- 4 oz Parmesan cheese
- 1 x 3-inch piece of fresh garlic bread
- 2 sprigs of rosemary

1 Peel and finely chop the onions and garlic, and add to a large Dutch oven over medium heat on the stove with the butter, bay, cayenne and 1 tablespoon of oil. Cook for 10 minutes, or until softened, stirring occasionally. Stir in the flour for 2 minutes, then gradually stir in the milk and add the mustard. Simmer for 10 minutes, or until thickened, then season to perfection and turn off the heat.

2 Meanwhile, cook the pasta in a large pot of boiling salted water according to the package instructions, then drain, reserving a generous cupful of starchy cooking water. Preheat the oven to 350°F.

3 Add the drained pasta to the sauce, grate in all the cheeses, then mix well and season to perfection, if needed. You don't want the sauce to be too thick at this point, so thin it with a little reserved cooking water, if needed.

4 Tear the garlic bread into a small food processor or blender, strip in the rosemary leaves, and blitz into coarse crumbs. Sprinkle over the pasta, then carefully transfer to the oven for 30 minutes, or until golden and bubbling. It'll retain its heat for a while, so will sit happily as part of a spread. Yum!

Grilled fries & rosemary salt

Serves 4 as a side | 30–40 minutes

2 lbs Yukon Gold potatoes

2 sprigs of rosemary

1 lemon

A grilled potato is a thing of joy. Yes, it requires a bit of love, but it's worth it. After cooking other things, simply shake the coals flat and get grilling.

1 Scrub the potatoes, then slice lengthwise into scant ½-inch-thick slabs, using a crinkle-cut knife for added texture, if you've got one. Toss with 2 tablespoons of olive oil and a pinch of black pepper.

2 To make a flavored salt, strip the rosemary leaves into a mortar and pestle, add 1 teaspoon of sea salt and pound until fine, then finely grate and mix in the lemon zest. Light the grill (pages 16–19).

3 Lay all the potatoes on the grate and cook with the lid on, vents open, for 40 minutes, or until cooked through and charred, turning regularly with tongs and spritzing with oil as you turn them. Transfer to a serving dish once done.

4 You can serve the fries right away, or grill them ahead and simply pop them on a baking sheet to heat through on the grill when you're ready. Sprinkle on some rosemary salt, to taste (saving the rest for another day), and tuck in. Great with my Pantry BBQ sauce (page 202), Chili sauce (page 204) or any of my flavored mayos (page 210), for epic dunking.

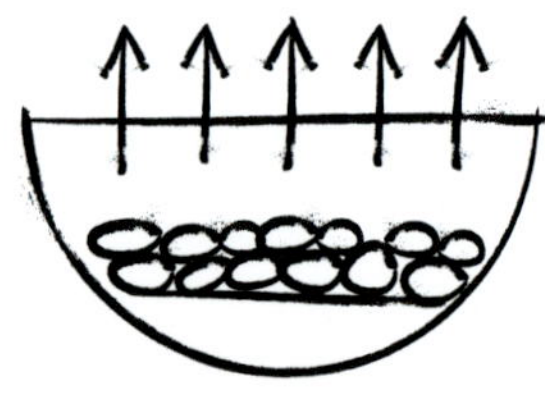

Flat

Beautiful burger buns

Makes 16 | 35 minutes, plus proofing & cooling

7 cups bread flour, plus extra for dusting

2¼ teaspoons instant or rapid-rise yeast

3 large eggs

1 generous tablespoon runny honey

optional: 2 tablespoons poppy, sesame or fennel seeds

1 Mix the flour, yeast and 1 tablespoon of sea salt in a large bowl and make a well in the middle. Beat in 2 eggs, then add 2⅓ cups of lukewarm water and the honey. Mix with a fork, then use clean hands to bring it together into a dough.

2 Knead on a clean, lightly floured surface for 5 minutes, or until smooth and elastic. Transfer to a lightly oiled bowl, cover with a clean, damp kitchen towel and let sit in a warm place for 1½ hours, or until doubled in size.

3 Turn the dough out of the bowl, punch it to knock out the air, then divide into 16 equal pieces. Shape the buns into tight rounds, arrange on two oiled baking sheets, leaving plenty of space between them, cover, and let sit for 30 minutes, or until doubled in size again.

4 Preheat the oven to 350°F. Depending on what finish you'd like, either lightly dust the bun tops with flour, or beat the remaining egg, eggwash the buns, and sprinkle with your chosen seeds, if using. Bake for 25 minutes, or until golden and the bottoms sound hollow when tapped, then let cool completely. Store in an airtight container for up to 3 days, or freeze until needed.

Easy swap: For tasty whole wheat buns, simply swap the bread flour for whole wheat bread flour and increase the water to 2½ cups.

My favorite focaccia

Serves 12 | 45 minutes, plus proofing

2¼ teaspoons instant or rapid-rise yeast

1 generous tablespoon runny honey

7 cups bread flour, plus extra for dusting

1 In a liquid measuring cup, whisk the yeast into 2½ cups of lukewarm water, stir in the honey, and let sit for 5 minutes. Whisk the flour with 1 teaspoon of sea salt in a large bowl and make a well in the middle.

2 Now, gradually pour the yeast mixture into the well, bringing in the flour from the outside to form a dough. Knead on a clean floured surface for 10 minutes, or until smooth and springy, picking the dough up and slapping it down as you go. Transfer to a lightly oiled bowl, cover with a clean, damp kitchen towel, and let sit in a warm place for 1 hour, or until doubled in size.

3 Lightly oil a deep baking pan (12 x 14 inches, or equivalent). Add the dough, pull and stretch it out to fill the pan, drizzle with 2 tablespoons of olive oil, then use your fingertips to gently push down and create lots of dips and wells. Sprinkle with a little salt, cover, and let sit for 1 hour, or until doubled in size again.

4 Preheat the oven to 425°F. Very carefully transfer the pan directly to the bottom of the oven (not on a rack) and bake for 25 minutes, or until golden and cooked through. Drizzle with at least 2 tablespoons of extra virgin olive oil, then remove form the pan and transfer to a board, ready to slice and serve.

Get ahead: You can do steps 1 and 2 a day ahead, and simply pop the dough into the fridge overnight.

Embellish it: Team this up with my Arrabiatta chicken drumsticks (page 140) for the most epic sandwich that's sure to go down a treat with your guests.

Charred flatbreads

Serves 4 | 5 minutes

1½ cups self-rising flour, plus extra for dusting (see note on page 84)

¾ cup plain yogurt

1 Light the grill (pages 16–19) and give the grate a really good brush to clean it – this will help prevent the breads from sticking.

2 In a large bowl, mix the flour with a little pinch of sea salt, the yogurt and 2 tablespoons of olive oil until it comes together as a dough. Divide equally into four, then roll and flatten out each piece on a clean floured surface until just over ⅛ inch thick, dusting well with flour as you go.

3 Grill on the hot zone for 1 minute on each side, or until charred, puffed up and cooked through, moving with tongs to the cooler zones, as needed.

Helpful hint: It's really easy to double or triple this recipe to feed a crowd.

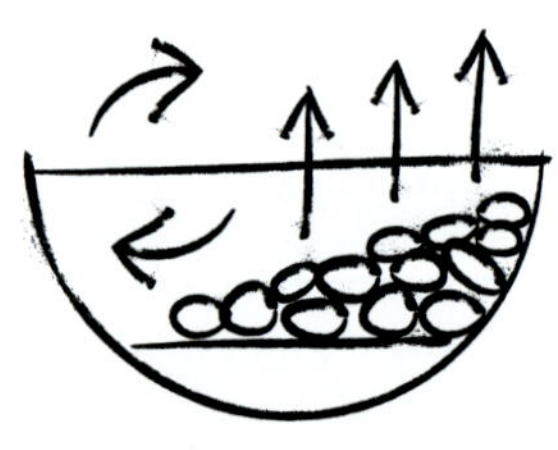
Graduated

Cooking sustainably & kitchen notes

Celebrate quality & seasonality

As is often the case in cooking, using quality ingredients really does make a difference to the success of the recipes. Wherever possible, I've tried to keep the number of ingredients under control, so I'm hoping that will give you the excuse to trade up where you can, buying the best veggies, fish or meat you can find. Also, remember that shopping in season means you get better value for money, and your ingredients will be even more delicious. When it comes to veg and fruit, remember to give everything a nice wash before you start cooking, especially if you're using stuff raw. Other ingredients that are noticeably more delicious when you choose the best quality are: oils and vinegars, sourdough, canned tomatoes, cheese, beans and chickpeas, jarred and tinned fish, chili crisp, sea salt, honey and coffee.

Focusing on fish & seafood

Fish and seafood are an incredibly delicious source of protein, but literally the minute they're caught they start to deteriorate in freshness, so you want to buy them as close to the day of your meal as you can – don't store them in the fridge for days, you're better off with frozen if that's the case. I recommend planning your fish and seafood dinners around your shopping days. Make sure you choose responsibly sourced fish and seafood – look for the MSC logo, or talk to your fishmonger and take their advice. Try to mix up your choices, choosing seasonal, sustainable options as they're available. If you can only find farmed fish, make sure you look for the ASC logo to ensure your fish is responsibly sourced. Jarred and tinned fish are great options, too, particularly when it comes to oily fish.

Meat & eggs

With meat, of course I'm going to endorse higher-welfare farming practices, like organic or free-range. Animals should be raised well, free to roam, display natural behaviors and live a stress-free healthy life. Like most things, you pay more for quality. I'm always a believer that if you take a couple of minutes to plan your weekly menus you can be clever about using cheaper cuts of meat, or you could try cooking some of my meat-reduced and meat-free dishes, which should give you the opportunity to trade up to quality proteins when you do choose them. Butchers can be very helpful – they can order stuff in especially for you and can ensure you have the exact weights you need. Unless essential to a recipe, I try not to specify egg sizes. Hens naturally lay a variety of sizes of egg, so look for mixed-size boxes when shopping to support the best possible welfare standards. Also, with eggs and anything containing egg, such as mayo, always choose free-range or organic.

Dial up your dairy

With staple dairy products, like milk, yogurt, cottage cheese and butter, please trade up to organic if you can. Every time you buy organic, you vote for a better food system that supports the highest standards of animal welfare, where both cows and land are well looked after.

Bigging up beans

Beans, legumes, chickpeas and lentils are a brilliant and tasty source of plant-based protein: they're budget-friendly, they live happily in the pantry for ages, they're easily accessible and they're full of fiber. Plus, they have a wonderful ability to take on flavors from all over the world, and growing beans is actually good for the planet. I've used them throughout this book, and would encourage you to embrace more of them in your cooking. Canned beans are great, but it's sometimes nice to trade up to jarred beans – they're normally at least twice the price but I'd say they're twice as delicious, too.

Maximizing flavor

In this book I use a lot of what I like to call "flavor shortcuts": widely available ingredients that allow you to add big bonus flavor, fast, often bolstering the taste of a dish in one super-charged ingredient. Much-loved pastes include rose harissa, miso, gochujang, tahini, chipotle chili paste and many curry pastes. Useful things in brine include jarred roasted red peppers, jarred sliced jalapeños, pickled walnuts, olives, cornichons and capers. Helpful things in oil: anchovies and sun-dried tomatoes. I love spices and blends like dukkah, dried red chili flakes, smoked paprika, Cajun seasoning and ground cinnamon, to name a few, as well as nuts, seeds and dried fruit for added crunch and texture; cracking condiments, such as mustards, Marmite, Worcestershire sauce, ketchup, HP sauce, mirin, chili oils and sauces like sriracha, mango chutney and marmalade, plus super sauces like hoisin, soy and Tabasco. These items guarantee flavor, educate your palate and save hours of time in preparation. Most are non-perishable, which means you're not under pressure to use them up super-quickly.

Bigging up fresh herbs

Fresh herbs are a gift to any cook. Instead of buying them, why not grow them yourself in the garden or in a pot on your windowsill? Herbs allow you to add amazing flavor and fragrance to a dish, without the need to over-season, which is good for everyone. They're also packed with all sorts of incredible qualities on the nutritional front – we like that. And don't forget dried herbs; they're non-perishable and super-convenient to have ready and raring to go in the pantry.

Fridge organization

When juggling space in the fridge, remember that raw meat and fish should be well wrapped and placed on the bottom shelf to avoid cross-contamination. Any food that is ready to eat, whether it's cooked or it doesn't need to be cooked, should be stored on a higher shelf.

The freezer is your friend

For busy people, without a doubt your freezer, if stocked correctly, is your closest ally. There are just a few basic rules when it comes to really utilizing it well. If you're batch-cooking, remember to let food cool thoroughly before freezing – break it down into portions so it cools quicker, and get it into the freezer within 2 hours. Make sure everything is well wrapped, and labeled for future reference. Thaw in the fridge before use, and use within 48 hours. If you've frozen cooked food, don't freeze it again after reheating or thawing it. You will see me using frozen veg (which I love!) in these recipes – it's super-convenient and widely available. Nutritionally speaking, freezing veg and fruit quickly after harvesting retains the nutritional value very efficiently, often trumping fresh equivalents that have been stuck in the supply chain for a while.

Grill & oven lovin'

All recipes were tested on a 22-inch charcoal kettle grill with two vents – all grills are different, so results may vary (for more info, see pages 16–17). Recipes that use an oven were tested in fan ovens in °C and then converted to °F for this book – find conversions for conventional and gas ovens online.

A note on nutrition

Our job is to make sure that Jamie can be super-creative, while also ensuring that all recipes meet our guidelines. Every book has a different brief, and *Grill* is a celebration of recipes you can cook up on your grill. It contains both fun meals for every day and those more indulgent weekend and special occasion dishes perfect for sharing with your loved ones. For clarity and so that you can make informed choices, we've presented easy-to-read nutrition info for each dish on pages 236–240 (displayed per serving). We also want to inspire a more sustainable way of eating, so have included lots of hero veg dishes and meat-free options in this book. Food is fun, joyful and creative – it gives us energy and plays a crucial role in keeping our bodies healthy. Remember, a nutritious, varied and balanced diet and regular exercise are the keys to a healthier lifestyle. We don't label foods as "good" or "bad" – there's a place for everything. We encourage an understanding of the difference between nutritious foods for everyday consumption and those to be enjoyed occasionally. For more info about our guidelines and how we analyze recipes, please visit jamieoliver.com/nutrition.

Rozzie Batchelar – Nutritionist, RNutr (food)

A bit about balance

Balance is key when it comes to eating well. Balance your plate right and keep your portion control in check, and you can be confident that you're giving yourself a great start on the path to good health. It's important to consume a variety of foods to ensure we get the nutrients our bodies need to stay healthy. You don't have to be spot-on every day – just try to get your balance right over the week. If you eat meat and fish, as a general guide for main meals you want at least two portions of fish a week, one of which should be oily. Split the rest of the week's main meals between brilliant plant-based meals, some poultry and a little red meat. An all-vegetarian diet can be perfectly healthy, too.

What's the balance?

The UK government's Eatwell Guide shows us what a healthy balance of food looks like. The figures below indicate the proportion of each food group that's recommended in a day.

THE FIVE FOOD GROUPS (UK)	PROPORTION
Vegetables & fruit	40%
Starchy carbohydrates (bread, rice, potatoes, pasta)	38%
Protein (lean meat, fish, eggs, beans, other non-dairy sources)	12%
Dairy foods, milk & dairy alternatives	8%
Unsaturated fats (such as oils)	1%
AND DON'T FORGET TO DRINK PLENTY OF WATER, TOO	

Try to only consume foods and drinks high in fat, salt or sugar occasionally.

Vegetables & fruit

To live a good, healthy life, vegetables and fruit should sit right at the heart of your diet. Veg and fruit come in all kinds of colors, shapes, sizes, flavors and textures, and contain different vitamins and minerals, which each play a part in keeping our bodies healthy and optimal, so variety is key. Eat the rainbow, mixing up your choices as much as you can and embracing the seasons so you're getting produce at its best and its most nutritious. As an absolute minimum, aim for at least 5 portions of fresh, frozen or canned veg and fruit every day of the week, enjoying more wherever possible. 80g/3 oz (or a large handful) counts as one portion. You can also count one 30g/1-oz portion of dried fruit, one 80g/3-oz portion of beans or legumes, and 150ml/about ⅔ cup of unsweetened veg or fruit juice per day.

Starchy carbohydrates

Carbs provide us with a large proportion of the energy needed to make our bodies move, and to ensure our organs have the fuel they need to function. When you can, choose fiber-rich whole grain and whole wheat varieties. 260g/9 oz is the recommended daily amount of carbohydrates for the average adult, with up to 90g/3 oz coming from total sugars, which includes natural sugars found in whole fruit, milk and milk products, and no more than 30g/1 oz of free sugars. Free sugars are those added to food and drink, including sugar found in honey, syrups, fruit juice and smoothies. Fiber is classified as a carbohydrate and is mainly found in plant-based foods such as whole grains, veg and fruit. It helps to keep our digestive systems healthy, control our blood-sugar levels and maintain healthy cholesterol levels. Adults should be aiming for at least 30g/1 oz of fiber each day.

Protein

Think of protein as the building blocks of our bodies – it's used for everything that's important to how we grow and repair. Try to vary your proteins to include more beans and pulses, two sources of sustainably sourced fish per week (one of which is oily) and reduce red and processed meat if your diet is high in these. Choose lean cuts of animal-based protein where you can. Beans, peas and lentils are great alternatives to meat because they're naturally low in fat and also contain fiber and some vitamins and minerals. Other nutritious protein sources include tofu, eggs, nuts and seeds. Variety is key! The requirement for an average female aged 19 to 50 is 45g/1½ oz per day, with 55g/2 oz for males in the same age bracket.

Dairy foods, milk & dairy alternatives

When eaten in the right amounts, this food group offers an amazing array of nutrients. Favor organic dairy milk and yogurt, and small amounts of cheese, in this category; the lower-fat varieties (with no added sugar) are equally brilliant and worth embracing. If opting for plant-based versions, it's great that we have choice, but it's really important to look for unsweetened fortified options that have added calcium, iodine and vitamin B12 in the ingredients list, to avoid missing out on the key nutrients provided by dairy milk.

Unsaturated fats

While we only need small amounts, we do require healthier fats. Choose unsaturated sources where you can, such as good-quality olive and liquid vegetable oils, nuts, seeds, avocado and omega-3 rich oily fish. Generally speaking, it's recommended that the average female has no more than 70g/2½ oz of fat per day, with less than 20g/¾ oz of that from saturated fat, and the average male no more than 90g/3 oz, with less than 30g/1 oz from saturated fat.

Drink plenty of water

To be the best you can be, stay hydrated. Water is essential to life, and to every function of the human body! In general, females aged 14 and over need at least 8 cups per day, and males in the same age bracket need at least 10 cups per day.

Energy & nutrition info

The average female needs 2,000 calories per day, while the average male needs 2,500. These figures are a rough guide, and what we eat needs to be considered in relation to factors like your age, build, lifestyle and activity levels.

A big thank you

Grilling for me is all about forging connections, and there is a wonderful bunch of brilliant people that I'm lucky enough to be connected with in all sorts of different ways, who have supported me in the creation of this beautiful book.

First up, and always leading the way, is my stellar food team. These are the people who live and breathe everything food-related that I do. They soak up inspiration, they share ideas, they help me develop and test recipes, support me on my photo shoots, and are just generally all-around brilliant friends. To my constant support and total trooper, the legend that is Ginny Rolfe, thank you for everything that you do. Big love to my right-hand man Hugo Harrison, and to rising star Isabella Leggett. Much respect for Ben Slater, now off doing his own thing. More respect and all the love to Sharon Sharpe for looking after us all, and to Rebecca Wheeldon and Tilly Wilson for being so helpful behind the scenes. My old-time food teamers, the OGs, Pete Begg and Bobby Sebire, I love you both dearly. Thank you.

I'm lucky to have a wonderful network of talented foodie people who step into the fray to support my core team when we need them to, and that's on everything from chipping into our photo shoots to endless recipe testing to make sure everything is spot-on. Big love to Isla Murray, Maddie Rix, Francesca Strange, Sophie Pryn, Chris Nam, Sophie Mackinnon, Steve Pooley, Holly Cowgill and Fran Paling. And to the brilliant runners who helped on our shoots, representing the next generation of talent, thank you Evie Rolfe and Daniel Martin.

Although grilling is often about big weekend cookouts, nutrition still has an important part to play, as it does in all the recipes I create. So big love, as always, to Rozzie Batchelar, for helping me make these recipes the best they can be without overstepping any marks! And thank you to Lucinda Cobb for guiding me when it comes to food safety, standards, farming and ethics.

On words, and all the supportive stuff around them, including working with the food team on the mammoth recipe testing process, big love to my extraordinary editor Rebecca Verity, to effervescent Jade Melling and the utterly grilliant Ruth Tebby, as well as the rest of the mighty editorial team.

And hand-in-hand with words goes design, so sharing much love and respect for my style icon, creative director James Verity, for these beautiful pages, and to the young talent that is Davina Mistry and to the rest of the JO design team.

We had a lot of fun shooting this book, and I think that's reflected in the stunning photography you see in these pages. It comes naturally to my dear friend David Loftus, so thank you, and big love to Richard Bowyer for brilliantly assisting Dave.

I must thank my publishers, the wonderful crew at Penguin Random House. There are so many talented people who work on my books, from creation and printing, to getting them out and seen in the world! I wish I got to spend more time with you all. Big respect to my dear friend, now big boss, Tom Weldon, and to the coolest publisher, the unstoppable Louise Moore. Thank you to Elizabeth Smith, dear Clare Parker, Becca Knight, Rebecca Ogden, Juliette Butler, Katherine Tibbals, Lee Motley, Nick Lowndes, Rachel Myers, Laura Garrod, Beth Stuart, Emma Carter, Hannah Padgham, Chris Wyatt, Tracy Orchard, Chantal Noel, Anjali Nathani, Kate Reiners, Tyra Burr, Joanna Whitehead, Lee-Anne Williams, Jessica Meredeen, George Dimopoulos, Amy Woollard, Sally Hargrave, Stuart Anderson, Jessica Adams, Caroline Newbury, Richard Rowlands and Carrie Anderson. Also to very precious Annie Lee, and to Rachel Malig, Jill Cole and Ruth Ellis.

And over at JO HQ, there is a wonderful bunch of brilliant people, busy doing all sorts of talented things, and they all come together to support these cookbooks. Thank you to the marketing crew, particularly Rosalind Godber and Clare Duffy. Thank you to comms queens Tamsyn Zeitsman and Lydia Waller. Thank you to Rich Herd and the VPU gang, and to Letitia Becher and her social team. Respect to Pamela Lovelock, Therese MacDermott and Mr John Dewar, as well as Timiko Cranwell and team. Thank you to Louise Holland, who goes above and beyond on a daily basis, as does my super-sharp EA Ali Solway. And huge love and gratitude to Zoe Collins x who was by my side at work for 25 years, through thick and thin, and is now off sharing her brilliance with the rest of the world. Lucky them.

There is a luscious complementary TV program celebrating all things grill, that I know you're going to enjoy, so huge thanks to that team. And in particular, the big trio, Sean Moxhay, Sam Beddoes and Katie Millard. As well as Jessica Honeyball, Niall Downing, Giulia Francalanci, Amanda Doig-Moore, Renzo Luzardo, Lulu Welford-Carroll, Prarthana Peterarulthas and all the brilliant crew. The talented Tobie Tripp has again over-delivered on the tunes, and love as always for the teams at Channel 4 and Fremantle. Shout out to Dan Cooper, Jon Folk and Sophie Gudat, talented, good folk from Weber who were brilliant collaborators on the show. Respect, hugs and love for Julia Bell.

And last but never least, the most important people in my life, and the ones who I am lucky enough to share food with every day, my darling family. Huge love for the woman who makes me laugh more than anyone else, my Jools, and to my brilliant children who I'm ever so proud of, Pops, Daisy, Petal, Buddy and River, love you guys. To Mum and Dad, thank you for being just the way you are, and thank you to the rest of the fam. Lastly, to my all-time favorite, Gennaro Contaldo, what would I do without you.

Nutrition

Chicken escalope, smoky bacon & pesto veg — PAGE 24

ENERGY	FAT	SAT FAT	PROTEIN	CARBS	SUGARS	SALT	FIBER
600kcal	36.9g	7.8g	51.7g	17.6g	7.3g	1.8g	8.7g

Perfect steak & chargrilled salad — PAGE 26

ENERGY	FAT	SAT FAT	PROTEIN	CARBS	SUGARS	SALT	FIBER
516kcal	24.2g	10.2g	48.1g	29g	22.3g	1g	7.4g

Lamb lollipops, whipped feta & pistachios — PAGE 28

ENERGY	FAT	SAT FAT	PROTEIN	CARBS	SUGARS	SALT	FIBER
644kcal	33.9g	16.4g	51.6g	35.9g	4g	2.1g	2.7g

Romesco cauliflower — PAGE 30

ENERGY	FAT	SAT FAT	PROTEIN	CARBS	SUGARS	SALT	FIBER
270kcal	13.1g	2.5g	10.8g	26.8g	12.1g	1g	7.4g

Quick beet mackerel — PAGE 32

ENERGY	FAT	SAT FAT	PROTEIN	CARBS	SUGARS	SALT	FIBER
251kcal	16.4g	4.4g	17.3g	9.1g	7.7g	1.2g	2.6g

Lemon-steamed fish & charred greens — PAGE 36

ENERGY	FAT	SAT FAT	PROTEIN	CARBS	SUGARS	SALT	FIBER
465kcal	30.9g	3.3g	36.9g	9.4g	5.8g	1.6g	6g

Seared carpaccio of beef — PAGE 38

ENERGY	FAT	SAT FAT	PROTEIN	CARBS	SUGARS	SALT	FIBER
524kcal	38.4g	11.6g	40.6g	4.1g	3.5g	2.3g	1.8g

Chicken skewers & Tuscan bread salad — PAGE 42

ENERGY	FAT	SAT FAT	PROTEIN	CARBS	SUGARS	SALT	FIBER
401kcal	14g	7g	35g	36.1g	11.9g	1.3g	5.4g

Grilled fish tacos & stone fruit salsa — PAGE 44

ENERGY	FAT	SAT FAT	PROTEIN	CARBS	SUGARS	SALT	FIBER
769kcal	39.1g	13.5g	51.6g	55g	18.4g	1.8g	3.9g

Herby eggplant & zingy feta flatbreads — PAGE 46

ENERGY	FAT	SAT FAT	PROTEIN	CARBS	SUGARS	SALT	FIBER
519kcal	30.8g	9.7g	16g	47.7g	19.2g	2.6g	11.6g

Jools' salmon niçoise — PAGE 48

ENERGY	FAT	SAT FAT	PROTEIN	CARBS	SUGARS	SALT	FIBER
607kcal	31.4g	5.8g	45.2g	39.3g	8.1g	1.8g	5.4g

Smashed lamb wraps — PAGE 50

ENERGY	FAT	SAT FAT	PROTEIN	CARBS	SUGARS	SALT	FIBER
728kcal	47.7g	14.1g	34g	41.7g	8.1g	3.7g	4.7g

Citrus chili tofu, greens & chickpea rice — PAGE 52

ENERGY	FAT	SAT FAT	PROTEIN	CARBS	SUGARS	SALT	FIBER
571kcal	11.1g	1.6g	25.1g	97.9g	18.1g	0.7g	8.2g

Sunshine stew & herb-stuffed sea bream — PAGE 54

ENERGY	FAT	SAT FAT	PROTEIN	CARBS	SUGARS	SALT	FIBER
385kcal	18.3g	2.1g	27g	32g	16.9g	1.1g	10g

Chicken shawarma — PAGE 56

ENERGY	FAT	SAT FAT	PROTEIN	CARBS	SUGARS	SALT	FIBER
434kcal	15.3g	4.3g	36.4g	38.3g	17.5g	1.8g	5.4g

Chicken & chorizo skewers — PAGE 60

ENERGY	FAT	SAT FAT	PROTEIN	CARBS	SUGARS	SALT	FIBER
238kcal	11.3g	3.3g	23.5g	11.5g	10.3g	1g	2g

Lamb kofta — PAGE 62

ENERGY	FAT	SAT FAT	PROTEIN	CARBS	SUGARS	SALT	FIBER
435kcal	25g	10.1g	29.9g	22.9g	4.9g	1.6g	2.3g

Halloumi & strawberry skewers — PAGE 64

ENERGY	FAT	SAT FAT	PROTEIN	CARBS	SUGARS	SALT	FIBER
544kcal	30.2g	19.2g	33.1g	33.6g	5.7g	3.8g	3.6g

Skewered sausages & creamy lentils — PAGE 66

ENERGY	FAT	SAT FAT	PROTEIN	CARBS	SUGARS	SALT	FIBER
689kcal	46.3g	19.6g	35g	32.8g	9.9g	2.7g	10.4g

Skewered sardines on toast
PAGE **68**

ENERGY	FAT	SAT FAT	PROTEIN	CARBS	SUGARS	SALT	FIBER
449kcal	27g	3.9g	27.9g	22.5g	2g	1.4g	2.4g

Dr Loftus' lamb kebabs
PAGE **70**

ENERGY	FAT	SAT FAT	PROTEIN	CARBS	SUGARS	SALT	FIBER
508kcal	41.4g	13.3g	25.8g	9g	5.9g	0.7g	3.9g

Shrimp skewers & ajoblanco sauce
PAGE **72**

ENERGY	FAT	SAT FAT	PROTEIN	CARBS	SUGARS	SALT	FIBER
583kcal	47g	7.5g	28.5g	14.7g	5.3g	1.9g	7.9g

Blushing bavette skewers & ssamjang
PAGE **74**

ENERGY	FAT	SAT FAT	PROTEIN	CARBS	SUGARS	SALT	FIBER
312kcal	17.4g	5.8g	28.2g	11.3g	10.2g	0.5g	2.7g

Sticky sriracha tofu
PAGE **76**

ENERGY	FAT	SAT FAT	PROTEIN	CARBS	SUGARS	SALT	FIBER
552kcal	18.6g	2.7g	21.1g	74.1g	24.6g	2.8g	0.5g

Peanutty chicken skewers
PAGE **78**

ENERGY	FAT	SAT FAT	PROTEIN	CARBS	SUGARS	SALT	FIBER
436kcal	25.9g	10.1g	46.4g	5.5g	3g	1g	1.3g

Spiced pork kebabs
PAGE **80**

ENERGY	FAT	SAT FAT	PROTEIN	CARBS	SUGARS	SALT	FIBER
256kcal	8.8g	3.1g	30g	15.8g	3.4g	0.8g	1.8g

Spiced chicken kebabs & butter sauce
PAGE **82**

ENERGY	FAT	SAT FAT	PROTEIN	CARBS	SUGARS	SALT	FIBER
602kcal	40.1g	19.4g	43g	20g	16.9g	1.5g	3.7g

Coconut & cilantro flatbread
PAGE **84**

ENERGY	FAT	SAT FAT	PROTEIN	CARBS	SUGARS	SALT	FIBER
303kcal	10.3g	8g	6.3g	49g	1.9g	1.1g	2.1g

Charred radicchio, orange & burrata salad
PAGE **88**

ENERGY	FAT	SAT FAT	PROTEIN	CARBS	SUGARS	SALT	FIBER
328kcal	23.3g	6.9g	10.7g	20.2g	15.8g	0.6g	4.3g

Grilled caponata
PAGE **90**

ENERGY	FAT	SAT FAT	PROTEIN	CARBS	SUGARS	SALT	FIBER
263kcal	13.6g	4.4g	10.5g	25.4g	7.9g	0.8g	4g

Med-style greens
PAGE **92**

ENERGY	FAT	SAT FAT	PROTEIN	CARBS	SUGARS	SALT	FIBER
125kcal	11.1g	1.6g	2.6g	5.3g	1.7g	1.2g	2g

Sriracha corn
PAGE **94**

ENERGY	FAT	SAT FAT	PROTEIN	CARBS	SUGARS	SALT	FIBER
153kcal	8.1g	0.8g	3.6g	19.8g	7.1g	0.2g	2g

Grilled green grain salad
PAGE **96**

ENERGY	FAT	SAT FAT	PROTEIN	CARBS	SUGARS	SALT	FIBER
296kcal	16.4g	3.6g	11.4g	25.4g	3.2g	0.3g	5.1g

Pickle potato salad
PAGE **98**

ENERGY	FAT	SAT FAT	PROTEIN	CARBS	SUGARS	SALT	FIBER
330kcal	13.5g	6.8g	8.6g	45.7g	8.1g	1.3g	3.4g

Herby grilled carrots & feta
PAGE **100**

ENERGY	FAT	SAT FAT	PROTEIN	CARBS	SUGARS	SALT	FIBER
248kcal	14.4g	4.8g	7.1g	24.6g	14.9g	1.8g	5.3g

Squash, sage & rice salad
PAGE **102**

ENERGY	FAT	SAT FAT	PROTEIN	CARBS	SUGARS	SALT	FIBER
499kcal	13.5g	1.8g	10.9g	89.8g	9.9g	0.4g	5.5g

Zucchini & ricotta salad
PAGE **104**

ENERGY	FAT	SAT FAT	PROTEIN	CARBS	SUGARS	SALT	FIBER
113kcal	8.4g	2.9g	4.9g	5.3g	4.7g	0.1g	1.6g

Yogurt pasta salad
PAGE **106**

ENERGY	FAT	SAT FAT	PROTEIN	CARBS	SUGARS	SALT	FIBER
376kcal	15.7g	4.2g	11.3g	51.5g	4.5g	0.1g	0.7g

Best-ever tomato salad
PAGE **108**

ENERGY	FAT	SAT FAT	PROTEIN	CARBS	SUGARS	SALT	FIBER
100kcal	6.6g	3.2g	4.8g	5.6g	5.5g	0.5g	1.7g

Charred squash & tahini chickpea salad PAGE 110

ENERGY	FAT	SAT FAT	PROTEIN	CARBS	SUGARS	SALT	FIBER
195kcal	7.5g	1.5g	7.1g	25.3g	11.3g	0.1g	5.8g

Beautiful Georgian-style stuffed eggplant PAGE 112

ENERGY	FAT	SAT FAT	PROTEIN	CARBS	SUGARS	SALT	FIBER
560kcal	51.8g	9.4g	10.1g	19g	9.3g	1.9g	8.5g

Glazed rum pineapple PAGE 116

ENERGY	FAT	SAT FAT	PROTEIN	CARBS	SUGARS	SALT	FIBER
309kcal	17.6g	8.8g	4.3g	28.3g	26.9g	0.2g	1.3g

Crispy bacon & sizzling sausages PAGE 121

ENERGY	FAT	SAT FAT	PROTEIN	CARBS	SUGARS	SALT	FIBER
235kcal	18.8g	6.8g	12.4g	4.1g	1.8g	1.3g	1.1g

Dotty coddled egg peppers PAGE 121

ENERGY	FAT	SAT FAT	PROTEIN	CARBS	SUGARS	SALT	FIBER
95kcal	5.9g	1.5g	7.1g	4.3g	4.1g	0.4g	2g

Tomato bread PAGE 122

ENERGY	FAT	SAT FAT	PROTEIN	CARBS	SUGARS	SALT	FIBER
83kcal	2g	0.3g	2.9g	13.2g	2.3g	0.2g	0.7g

Bubbling baked beans PAGE 122

ENERGY	FAT	SAT FAT	PROTEIN	CARBS	SUGARS	SALT	FIBER
168kcal	0.7g	0.1g	10g	32.1g	8.9g	1.3g	8g

Stuffed mushrooms PAGE 122

ENERGY	FAT	SAT FAT	PROTEIN	CARBS	SUGARS	SALT	FIBER
104kcal	7.1g	4.4g	7.6g	3.4g	2.3g	0.8g	1.1g

Corn fritters PAGE 124

ENERGY	FAT	SAT FAT	PROTEIN	CARBS	SUGARS	SALT	FIBER
342kcal	13g	4.1g	13.3g	44.3g	5.3g	1.5g	2g

BBQ baked beans PAGE 126

ENERGY	FAT	SAT FAT	PROTEIN	CARBS	SUGARS	SALT	FIBER
188kcal	5g	0.8g	6.8g	26.9g	15.8g	0.7g	6.4g

Grilled black pepper peaches PAGE 128

ENERGY	FAT	SAT FAT	PROTEIN	CARBS	SUGARS	SALT	FIBER
446kcal	16.1g	10.2g	12.7g	64.2g	40.5g	0.7g	3.8g

Halloumi fritters PAGE 130

ENERGY	FAT	SAT FAT	PROTEIN	CARBS	SUGARS	SALT	FIBER
254kcal	13.4g	6.3g	15g	38.3g	6.2g	2.2g	1.9g

Barbecued meat chilli PAGE 134

ENERGY	FAT	SAT FAT	PROTEIN	CARBS	SUGARS	SALT	FIBER
390kcal	20.6g	7.4g	39.6g	11.8g	5.8g	1.2g	4.2g

Juicy pork belly, fennel & orange salad PAGE 136

ENERGY	FAT	SAT FAT	PROTEIN	CARBS	SUGARS	SALT	FIBER
542kcal	42.2g	13.6g	33.4g	8.2g	5.6g	1.5g	2.6g

Gnarly sirloin roast with salsa, rice & beans PAGE 138

ENERGY	FAT	SAT FAT	PROTEIN	CARBS	SUGARS	SALT	FIBER
416kcal	15g	5.9g	30.5g	41.6g	7g	0.9g	3.4g

Arrabiatta chicken drumsticks PAGE 140

ENERGY	FAT	SAT FAT	PROTEIN	CARBS	SUGARS	SALT	FIBER
339kcal	15.6g	4g	29.2g	12.2g	10.4g	1g	3.6g

Classic leg of lamb PAGE 144

ENERGY	FAT	SAT FAT	PROTEIN	CARBS	SUGARS	SALT	FIBER
487kcal	29.5g	12.2g	44.2g	11.5g	9.2g	1g	3.3g

Herby grilled veg & halloumi skewers PAGE 146

ENERGY	FAT	SAT FAT	PROTEIN	CARBS	SUGARS	SALT	FIBER
516kcal	29.1g	7.7g	17.1g	49.6g	18.1g	1.4g	7.7g

Grilled chili & lemon chicken PAGE 148

ENERGY	FAT	SAT FAT	PROTEIN	CARBS	SUGARS	SALT	FIBER
353kcal	20.1g	5g	39.9g	3.1g	1.1g	0.7g	0.6g

Herby leg of lamb & creamy beans PAGE 152

ENERGY	FAT	SAT FAT	PROTEIN	CARBS	SUGARS	SALT	FIBER
468kcal	23.2g	8.7g	35.8g	26.7g	3.8g	0.9g	7.5g

Pulled beef tacos
PAGE **154**

ENERGY	FAT	SAT FAT	PROTEIN	CARBS	SUGARS	SALT	FIBER
456kcal	23.1g	6.6g	26.6g	35.9g	13.6g	2.1g	4.5g

Pomegranate & harissa chicken
PAGE **156**

ENERGY	FAT	SAT FAT	PROTEIN	CARBS	SUGARS	SALT	FIBER
395kcal	20.8g	5g	39.6g	12.8g	11.6g	0.8g	1g

Ultimate pork ribs – BBQ sauce glaze
PAGE **158**

ENERGY	FAT	SAT FAT	PROTEIN	CARBS	SUGARS	SALT	FIBER
354kcal	23.4g	10.4g	22.2g	13.6g	12g	2.8g	0.6g

Ultimate pork ribs – hoisin glaze
PAGE **158**

ENERGY	FAT	SAT FAT	PROTEIN	CARBS	SUGARS	SALT	FIBER
387kcal	22.2g	10.2g	21.8g	25.0g	22.8g	2.8g	0.6g

Ultimate pork ribs – mango chutney glaze
PAGE **158**

ENERGY	FAT	SAT FAT	PROTEIN	CARBS	SUGARS	SALT	FIBER
366kcal	22.6g	10.2g	22.2g	18.8g	16.2g	3.3g	1g

Buddy's chicken Caesar
PAGE **160**

ENERGY	FAT	SAT FAT	PROTEIN	CARBS	SUGARS	SALT	FIBER
593kcal	28.3g	9.3g	57.7g	27.1g	10.3g	2.6g	6.7g

Veggie gumbo
PAGE **164**

ENERGY	FAT	SAT FAT	PROTEIN	CARBS	SUGARS	SALT	FIBER
270kcal	10.2g	1.8g	11.6g	35.8g	11.6g	1.4g	9g

Fruity pork chops & grilled potatoes
PAGE **166**

ENERGY	FAT	SAT FAT	PROTEIN	CARBS	SUGARS	SALT	FIBER
709kcal	37.3g	13g	15.2g	48.7g	17.5g	0.9g	4.5g

Super surf & turf mixed grill
PAGE **168**

ENERGY	FAT	SAT FAT	PROTEIN	CARBS	SUGARS	SALT	FIBER
594kcal	36g	11.7g	39g	27.3g	5.1g	2.2g	3.7g

Duck legs & plum sauce
PAGE **170**

ENERGY	FAT	SAT FAT	PROTEIN	CARBS	SUGARS	SALT	FIBER
761kcal	23.6g	7g	50.3g	93.1g	18.1g	2.4g	13.4g

Mint & chili zucchini
PAGE **174**

ENERGY	FAT	SAT FAT	PROTEIN	CARBS	SUGARS	SALT	FIBER
32kcal	2.4g	0.4g	0.9g	2.3g	1.8g	0g	0.6g

Burnt butter labneh
PAGE **175**

ENERGY	FAT	SAT FAT	PROTEIN	CARBS	SUGARS	SALT	FIBER
163kcal	13.8g	8.6g	4g	5.1g	3.8g	0.5g	1.8g

Anchovies & orange
PAGE **175**

ENERGY	FAT	SAT FAT	PROTEIN	CARBS	SUGARS	SALT	FIBER
11kcal	0.5g	0.1g	1.3g	0.4g	0.4g	0.7g	0g

Halloumi & apricots
PAGE **175**

ENERGY	FAT	SAT FAT	PROTEIN	CARBS	SUGARS	SALT	FIBER
184kcal	13.3g	6.9g	9.7g	7.1g	6.1g	1.1g	1g

Baba ganoush
PAGE **176**

ENERGY	FAT	SAT FAT	PROTEIN	CARBS	SUGARS	SALT	FIBER
53kcal	3.1g	0.5g	2g	5.1g	2.3g	0g	2.9g

Sweet peppers & capers
PAGE **176**

ENERGY	FAT	SAT FAT	PROTEIN	CARBS	SUGARS	SALT	FIBER
17kcal	0.3g	0.1g	0.8g	3g	2.9g	0.2g	1.2g

Tear & share flatbread
PAGE **176**

ENERGY	FAT	SAT FAT	PROTEIN	CARBS	SUGARS	SALT	FIBER
211kcal	3.8g	1.4g	6.7g	39.9g	2.7g	0.8g	1.8g

Paprika pulled pork
PAGE **178**

ENERGY	FAT	SAT FAT	PROTEIN	CARBS	SUGARS	SALT	FIBER
448kcal	33.8g	10.8g	36.2g	0g	0g	0.5g	0g

Gravy cheeseburgers
PAGE **182**

ENERGY	FAT	SAT FAT	PROTEIN	CARBS	SUGARS	SALT	FIBER
764kcal	46.5g	13.3g	41.9g	44.3g	10g	2.9g	3.9g

Miso mushroom burgers
PAGE **184**

ENERGY	FAT	SAT FAT	PROTEIN	CARBS	SUGARS	SALT	FIBER
310kcal	7g	1.1g	11.9g	49.1g	14.4g	2.7g	4.7g

Lamb moussaka burgers
PAGE **188**

ENERGY	FAT	SAT FAT	PROTEIN	CARBS	SUGARS	SALT	FIBER
588kcal	29.3g	14.9g	40.1g	41.4g	10.4g	2.7g	4.6g

Sesame chicken burgers
PAGE **190**

ENERGY	FAT	SAT FAT	PROTEIN	CARBS	SUGARS	SALT	FIBER
438kcal	12.7g	3.1g	38.2g	42.1g	12.1g	1.7g	4.5g

Blue cheese pork burgers
PAGE **192**

ENERGY	FAT	SAT FAT	PROTEIN	CARBS	SUGARS	SALT	FIBER
742kcal	46.2g	15.9g	40.2g	40.5g	11.4g	2.3g	3.2g

Beet & feta bean burgers
PAGE **194**

ENERGY	FAT	SAT FAT	PROTEIN	CARBS	SUGARS	SALT	FIBER
455kcal	9.1g	3.2g	21.4g	71.1g	16.4g	1.8g	10.8g

Shrimp toast burgers
PAGE **196**

ENERGY	FAT	SAT FAT	PROTEIN	CARBS	SUGARS	SALT	FIBER
380kcal	8.6g	1.4g	32g	42.6g	12g	1.7g	2.9g

Chorizo fish burgers
PAGE **198**

ENERGY	FAT	SAT FAT	PROTEIN	CARBS	SUGARS	SALT	FIBER
676kcal	38.2g	9.8g	43.5g	39.9g	9.6g	1.9g	4.3g

Pantry BBQ sauce (per tablespoon)
PAGE **202**

ENERGY	FAT	SAT FAT	PROTEIN	CARBS	SUGARS	SALT	FIBER
34kcal	0.6g	0.2g	0.5g	6.4g	5.9g	0.4g	0.2g

Chili sauce (per tablespoon)
PAGE **204**

ENERGY	FAT	SAT FAT	PROTEIN	CARBS	SUGARS	SALT	FIBER
20kcal	0.9g	0g	0.3g	3.2g	2.9g	0.2g	0.3g

Salsa verde
PAGE **206**

ENERGY	FAT	SAT FAT	PROTEIN	CARBS	SUGARS	SALT	FIBER
60kcal	5.5g	0.8g	1.5g	0.9g	0.6g	0.7g	0.3g

Salsa rossa piccante
PAGE **208**

ENERGY	FAT	SAT FAT	PROTEIN	CARBS	SUGARS	SALT	FIBER
71kcal	3.6g	0.5g	1.9g	8.4g	6.9g	0.5g	2.8g

Homemade mayo (per tablespoon)
PAGE **210**

ENERGY	FAT	SAT FAT	PROTEIN	CARBS	SUGARS	SALT	FIBER
122kcal	13.5g	2g	0.1g	0.1g	0g	0g	0g

Smoky ketchup (per tablespoon)
PAGE **212**

ENERGY	FAT	SAT FAT	PROTEIN	CARBS	SUGARS	SALT	FIBER
33kcal	1g	0g	0.5g	4.9g	4.4g	0.2g	1g

Crispy chickpea hummus
PAGE **214**

ENERGY	FAT	SAT FAT	PROTEIN	CARBS	SUGARS	SALT	FIBER
82kcal	4g	0.6g	3.9g	8g	0.4g	0.2g	2.6g

Charred chili oil (per tablespoon)
PAGE **216**

ENERGY	FAT	SAT FAT	PROTEIN	CARBS	SUGARS	SALT	FIBER
56kcal	6g	0.9g	0.2g	0.4g	0.4g	0.2g	0.1g

Bay salt (per teaspoon)
PAGE **218**

ENERGY	FAT	SAT FAT	PROTEIN	CARBS	SUGARS	SALT	FIBER
3kcal	0.2g	0g	0.3g	0.5g	0g	1.4g	0.3g

Mega mac 'n' cheese
PAGE **220**

ENERGY	FAT	SAT FAT	PROTEIN	CARBS	SUGARS	SALT	FIBER
419kcal	19g	10.3g	20.6g	55g	9.3g	0.9g	2.7g

Grilled fries & rosemary salt
PAGE **222**

ENERGY	FAT	SAT FAT	PROTEIN	CARBS	SUGARS	SALT	FIBER
247kcal	7.1g	0.9g	5.1g	43.3g	1.5g	1g	3.3g

Beautiful burger buns
PAGE **224**

ENERGY	FAT	SAT FAT	PROTEIN	CARBS	SUGARS	SALT	FIBER
241kcal	1.9g	0.4g	8.8g	50.6g	1.4g	1.3g	2g

My favorite focaccia
PAGE **226**

ENERGY	FAT	SAT FAT	PROTEIN	CARBS	SUGARS	SALT	FIBER
305kcal	3.4g	0.5g	9.8g	62.8g	1.1g	0.3g	2.6g

Charred flatbreads
PAGE **228**

ENERGY	FAT	SAT FAT	PROTEIN	CARBS	SUGARS	SALT	FIBER
252kcal	8.6g	2g	6.1g	39.8g	2.6g	0.8g	1.6g

Index

Recipes marked **V** are suitable for vegetarians; in some instances you'll need to swap in a vegetarian alternative to cheese such as Parmesan.

A

B

C

D

E

J

K

L

M

N

O

P

Q

R

S

T

U

V

W

Y

Z

For a quick reference list of all the vegetarian, vegan, dairy-free and gluten-free recipes in this book, visit: jamieoliver.com/BBQ/special-diets

---

The Jamie Oliver collection

1 The Naked Chef *1999*

2 The Return of the Naked Chef *2000*

3 Happy Days with the Naked Chef *2001*

4 Jamie's Kitchen *2002*

5 Jamie's Dinners *2004*

6 Jamie's Italy *2005*

7 Cook with Jamie *2006*

8 Jamie at Home *2007*

9 Jamie's Food Revolution *2008*

10 Jamie's America *2009*

11 Jamie Oliver's Food Escapes *2010*

12 Jamie Oliver's Meals in Minutes *2010*

13 Jamie's Great Britain *2011*

14 Jamie's 15-Minute Meals *2012*

15 Save with Jamie *2013*

16 Jamie's Comfort Food *2014*

17 Everyday Super Food *2015*

18 Super Food Family Classics *2016*

19 Jamie Oliver's Christmas Cookbook *2016*

20 5 Ingredients – Quick & Easy Food *2017*

21 Jamie Cooks Italy *2018*

22 Jamie's Friday Night Feast Cookbook *2018*

23 Ultimate Veg *2019*

24 7 Ways *2020*

25 Together *2021*

26 ONE *2022*

27 5 Ingredients Mediterranean *2023*

28 Simply Jamie *2024*

29 Easy Air Fryer *2025*

30 Eat Yourself Healthy *2025*

31 Grill *2026*

Hungry for more?

For handy nutrition advice, as well as videos, features, hints, tricks and tips on all sorts of different subjects, loads of brilliant recipes, plus much more, check out

JAMIEOLIVER.COM

Photography by David Loftus

Design by Jamie Oliver Limited

First published in the UK by Penguin Michael Joseph, part of the Penguin Random House group of companies.

Published in Canada by Appetite by Random House®, a division of Penguin Random House LLC.

Library and Archives Canada Cataloguing in Publication is available upon request.
ISBN: 978-0-525-61377-0
eBook ISBN: 978-0-525-61378-7

Color reproduction by Altaimage Ltd

Printed in China

The authorized representative in the EU for product safety and compliance is
Penguin Random House Ireland, Morrison Chambers, 32 Nassau Street,
Dublin D02 YH68, Ireland, https://eu-contact.penguin.ie

Published in Canada by Appetite by Random House®,
a division of Penguin Random House Canada Limited.
320 Front Street West, Suite 1400
Toronto, Ontario, M5V 3B6, Canada

penguinrandomhouse.ca

jamieoliver.com

First Canadian Edition

10 9 8 7 6 5 4 3 2 1

Penguin Random House is committed to a sustainable future for our business, our readers and our planet. This book is made from Forest Stewardship Council® certified paper

Big love
Thank you for buying my cookbook – by doing so you're contributing to my Ministry of Food Programme, which is on a mission to teach 1 million people to cook by 2030.
FIND OUT MORE: JAMIEOLIVER.COM/MOF